THE CATEGORY MANAGEMENT HANDBOOK

Category management is one of the biggest contributors of commercial value in the area of procurement and supply chain. With a proven track record of successful delivery since the early 1990s, it helps organisations gather and analyse key data about their procurement spend before subsequently creating and delivering value-adding strategies that change the value proposition from supply chains. The aim of category management is to find long-term breakthrough strategies that help lift an organisation's commercial performance to a new level. Because of its strategic long-term orientation and complex execution, category management has long been the preserve of commercial consulting companies – in effect a 'black box' toolkit shrouded in expensive methodologies.

This practical handbook lifts the lid on category management by providing readers with a step-by-step process and established toolkit that allows them a 'do-it-yourself' approach. Each activity is presented as a simple tool or technique for practitioners to apply to their own organisations. To support each activity, easy-to-use templates and checklists have been provided, together with simple but practical hints and tips for implementation.

This handbook is a 'must read' for all procurement and supply-chain managers looking to find significant improvements in their organisations. Its practical approach cuts through long-winded consultant-speak and provides an easy-to-use practical toolkit for everyday application.

Andrea Cordell is a well-known international speaker and author on strategy, negotiation and procurement-related matters. She has worked in senior positions at several global organisations and is currently the managing director of Cordie Ltd, a leading sales and procurement training and consulting company.

Ian Thompson is a leading authority on category management, having worked in a number of senior positions at global organisations and consulting companies. He is currently one of the founding directors of Cordie Ltd, a leading sales and procurement training and consulting company.

THE CATEGORY MANAGEMENT HANDBOOK

Andrea Cordell and Ian Thompson

Routledge
Taylor & Francis Group

LONDON AND NEW YORK

First published 2018
by Routledge
2 Park Square, Milton Park, Abingdon, Oxon OX14 4RN

and by Routledge
711 Third Avenue, New York, NY 10017

Routledge is an imprint of the Taylor & Francis Group, an informa business

© 2018 Andrea Cordell and Ian Thompson

British Library Cataloguing-in-Publication Data
A catalog record for this book is available from the British Library

Library of Congress Cataloguing-in-Publication Data
Names: Cordell, Andrea, 1965– author. | Thompson, Ian, 1967– author.
Title: The category management handbook / Andrea Cordell and Ian Thompson.
Description: 1 Edition. | New York : Routledge, 2018. | Includes bibliographical references and index.
Identifiers: LCCN 2017053080 (print) | LCCN 2018009983 (ebook) |
ISBN 9781351239585 (eBook) | ISBN 9780815375531 (hardback : alk. paper) |
ISBN 9780815375517 (pbk. : alk. paper)
Subjects: LCSH: Purchasing. | Business logistics. | Project management.
Classification: LCC HF5437 (ebook) | LCC HF5437 .C67 2018 (print) |
DDC 658.7/2—dc23
LC record available at https://lccn.loc.gov/2017053080

ISBN: 978-0-8153-7553-1 (hbk)
ISBN: 978-0-8153-7551-7 (pbk)
ISBN: 978-1-351-23958-5 (ebk)

Typeset in Bembo
by Apex CoVantage, LLC

CONTENTS

Contents

FIGURES

TEMPLATES

ACKNOWLEDGEMENTS

We would like to thank our corporate clients, colleagues and friends who have worked with us over recent years, tirelessly striving for improved business value through category management. You have been the inspiration for this handbook.

We would also like to acknowledge the students at our five Cordie study centres who have studied both the good (and the bad) aspects of category management as part of their ongoing professional development. This handbook is for you.

Our final words of gratitude go to Samantha Wheeler and Ruth Paskins for their patience in assisting us with this labour of love and to Al O'Reilly, Tracey Webster and the rest of the Cordie team for their enduring support with our training services.

ABOUT THE AUTHORS

Andrea Cordell

Andrea is the managing director of Cordie Ltd, a leading sales, procurement and supply-chain training organisation. While she is well known for her enthusiastic and interactive public speaking style, her specialist subject is the human dynamics and hypnotic language surrounding commercial relationships and, in particular, subliminal linguistics.

Andrea has an MBA from Henley Business School and is an NLP Master, as well as a licenced MBTI® Assessor and a registered EQ Tester. She is a fellow of both the Institute of Sales Management and CIPS.

Ian Thompson

Ian is one of the directors and cofounders of Cordie Ltd, as well as a fellow of both the Institute of Leadership and Management and CIPS. He currently leads commercial training programmes on a worldwide basis, where his specialist subjects include category management, strategic sourcing and public procurement regulation.

Prior to establishing Cordie, Ian led sourcing teams in several large blue-chip organisations and before that worked as a chartered engineer on major infrastructure projects.

Ian has written three procurement textbooks and has an MBA from the University of Birmingham. He has set up five successful CIPS study centres and helped Cordie twice win the United Kingdom's national training awards for 'outstanding training delivery'.

Other books by Andrea and Ian include:
* *The Procurement Models Handbook*
* *The Negotiation Handbook*
* *Emotional Intelligence and Negotiation*

INTRODUCTION

For the last two decades we have witnessed countless consulting practices and their client organisations promote the benefits of implementing category management. As a process it has been heralded as the procurement 'panacea' that delivers huge efficiency savings and business-wide benefits. It's the one methodology that truly operates cross-functionally and works systematically through a strategic process to deliver exceptional outcomes.

Ironically, there is very little published material about category management – and what has been published remains shrouded in consultant-speak. As a result, organisations are left either to fend for themselves (and there are some really sub-optimal examples of category management out there) or to employ expensive consultants to deliver fancy overengineered toolkits that never really get implemented.

This is what drove us to write this handbook: to offer a simple practitioners' guide that lifts the lid on category management and increases the application of best practice in the procurement field. When done well, we have seen category management deliver exceptional results, and so we hope this practical handbook helps inspire you to take up category management and deliver great things for your organisation!

Background

The origins of category management track back to the proliferation of marketing and merchandising strategies in the 1980s. Back then, multibrand fast-moving consumer goods (FMCG) manufacturers realised the benefits of grouping their products into 'categories' of associated offerings in order to maximise their market position and to drive synergies across various retail channels and consumer groups. This association of products and classification of customer groupings became known as category management and the natural flow through to supply-chain operations quickly followed on.

Since then, category management has expanded beyond FMCG and become intrinsically focused on buy-side supply markets. Through the 1990s, procurement consultancies picked up on the added value of category management and 'process engineered' the approach so that it could apply to indirect, as well as direct, spend. It quickly became associated with large strategic analysis and sourcing toolkits. As authors, we were introduced to category management a little over 20 years ago and have seen both the positive benefits and the downsides of processes like these.

When applied well, considerable business benefits were realised – far more than any typical procurement approach – and category management has grabbed considerable management attention. However, sometimes it didn't go so well, and the only winners were the consultants who collected their overinflated pay cheques.

More recently however category management has matured and become grounded in everyday business practice, but it still remains a 'black box' and one of the preserves of the consultancies.

This is what this handbook is about. Category management is a well-established, proven methodology that delivers business benefits. However, it's not rocket science and you don't need expensive consultants to deliver the mystique for you.

What is category management?

Category management is a continuous process of gathering, analysing and reviewing market data in order to create and execute spend strategies that deliver long-term business benefits.

Let's look at this definition closer by eliminating other activities that sometimes get confused with category management. First and most importantly, category management is different from sourcing. So many people get this muddled (including some of the so-called leading professional bodies), and this is a major inhibitor of the strategic creativity of potential solutions. While sourcing (if done well) can have many of the same activities, it is only a one-dimensional approach to category management. Category management can include sourcing but also considers a whole load of other potential solutions, including make versus buy, outsourcing, insourcing, offshoring/reshoring, renegotiation, forward/backward integration, supplier relationship management, new product development, acquisitions and joint ventures, to name but a few. As such, category management should deliver significantly more value than sourcing, which in turn delivers more value than buying, as illustrated in Figure I.1.

Similarly, category management is not a 'project'. If you haven't done it before, then obviously it has a clear beginning, but it shouldn't have an end. To make life easier you might organise responsibilities into category management teams and have them run various delivery 'projects' against a time frame, but this is merely for convenience. True category management is iterative, constantly evolving and transitioning from one generation to another; the process is cyclical and by definition never ending.

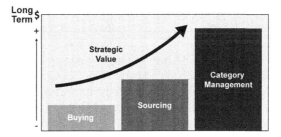

Figure I.1 Strategic value of category management

Finally, category management is not a spend report (i.e. it does not accept organisational spending as is); it's a *strategy* that delivers business benefits based on *changing* the way expenditure and resources are managed.

Key principles

There are six key cornerstones of successful category management:

1 **Customer focus** – Everything in category management must be customer led, with targets and objectives being focused on business-wide priorities (what we later refer to as 'business requirements'). Where the customer is internal (e.g. areas of indirect spend), then this is about excellent stakeholder engagement and a service-oriented philosophy. Where the customer is external (e.g. areas of direct spend), then the business requirements will need to be a carefully considered trade-off between serving business needs and delighting customers. Business requirements form the underlying bedrock of all category management, and without a thorough analysis and understanding of these, any category management solution is most likely to be suboptimal. You will consider these in more detail in the research stage of our category management process (refer to Stage 2, Activity 8).

2 **Changing the status quo** – Everything in category management is about change (and improvement). Put simply, if you don't want to change then don't engage in category management! Perhaps more fundamentally, category management is about 'breakthrough' thinking – that is, seeking out and exploiting new opportunities to make fundamental leaps of improvement.

3 **Process thinking** – As already mentioned, category management is a cyclical process of sequential activities. By sequencing these activities into a step-by-step process, category management teams can be systematic in their approach to strategy development and implementation. Governance can also be created, giving the opportunity for business controls and peer review/challenge at appropriate places.

4 **Cross-functional approach** – Fundamental to successful category management is the business-wide approach. Here stakeholders are not merely

'consultees'; they become actively engaged in leading and managing the category activities. It moves the category management process away from functional procurement and embeds it as a business process of change.

5   **Facts and data driven** – All analysis, strategies and decisions should be based on a strong foundation of facts and data. This helps to remove subjectivity, bias and organisational politics. When faced with well-informed market intelligence, the business is able to buy into strategies for change.

6   **Continuous improvement** – Unlike a project, category management does not have a defined end. The process of activities may conclude after one category strategy has been successfully implemented, but this is the trigger for the next generation (iteration) of category management to evolve. In other words, the process is cyclical, constantly seeking out better and better solutions to manage each spend category.

Process and governance

There are many different formats for the category management process, with no definitive guidance on which process is best. The authors have worked with clients that have three-stage category management processes, others that have 12-stage processes and many in between these extremes. There isn't a right or wrong number of stages.

In this book we adopt a 'classic' five-stage category management process (see Figure I.2). We have done this for several reasons, but mostly for convenience. Primarily, five-stage processes seem to be the most popular across businesses. Having five distinct stages keeps the structure relatively simple and groups activities into a natural sequence; any less than this can make the process stages seem too large, while more than this seems to overcomplicate matters. We have grouped individual activities logically into this five-stage structure based on our practical experience of working within and facilitating category teams through a wide range of categories throughout the world.

In addition to a distinct number of process stages, there are specific 'gateways' that sit between each stage. These gateways provide excellent check steps or review points to monitor progression through the process. It is generally advisable to insert some form of governance around these gateways. More formal 'mature' category management processes treat these gateways as 'go/no-go' decision milestones, thus maintaining focus and a degree of project management behind each process iteration.

While we are fans of this relatively simple five-stage process, it is worth drawing a comparison with other published methodologies. For example, the United Kingdom's Chartered Institute of Procurement & Supply (CIPS) recently created

Figure I.2   Category management process

its own category management model based on a circular cycle of activities. This process has many similarities to the process we follow in this handbook, albeit that we have simplified our overall approach to make it more generic across multiple industry sectors.

Two of the key features of this CIPS category management model that differ from our approach include (1) the alignment of category strategy and execution around the key activities of a sourcing process, and (2) a specific emphasis on postaward supplier management and continuous improvement.

The confusion between sourcing and category management is a common occurrence throughout the industry. It is understandable that CIPS (and other procurement consultancies) base their category management models on sourcing – they do after all concentrate on selling procurement services – but this approach is far too limiting and denies the true strategic intention that sits behind category management. By mistakenly including sourcing and supplier management processes in a category management process, there is a major presumption that all spend strategies will require a sourcing solution. The reality is that these strategies might not require any sourcing whatsoever and so to automatically build a sourcing stage into the category management process could be extremely limiting on the variety of strategic options that the category management process creates.

The five-stage category management process that we detail in this book has a far broader business appeal than just procurement. It leaves 'no stone unturned' in its attempt to find strategic solutions for each category. While sourcing a new offering from the supply market could be one option, we strongly encourage you to think more broadly than this and pursue a variety of ideas and options in order to deliver sustained value to your business.

Presentation of this handbook

This handbook has been subdivided into five key sections, each representing one of the stages of our category management process. Within each section we explain the tools and techniques that you are likely to use. Each tool or technique is presented in graphical form with accompanying commentary, in the following format:

- **Overview** – A brief introduction of the tool/technique and an explanation of how it fits in the category management process.
- **Elements** – A description of the key components of the tool/technique and how they are applied.
- **So what?** – A practical guide as to how the tool/technique is generally used on an operational level and what it delivers for organisations.
- **Category management application** – Suggestions as to how the tool/technique can be applied specifically as part of an overall category management approach and the benefits that it will bring.
- **Limitations** – An open and even-handed critique of the tool/technique.
- **Template** – A reference to the corresponding template that accompanies each tool/technique for your easy application.

STAGE 1

Initiation

Overview and benefits of this stage

Why start with governance, and why not simply 'get on' with category management?

There is a desire within many organisations to 'rush' into category management and to 'execute at pace'. This is ill-conceived if an organisation is looking to make major changes and create significant lasting benefits. It is logical to assume that most of the obvious opportunities for commercial improvement have already been taken; otherwise, why engage in category management? So the main reason why organisations are adopting category management should be because they are looking for a step change in delivery.

In category management this is referred to as *breakthrough* thinking. Category management has the ability to bring together a wide number of stakeholders and to get the organisation thinking and behaving strategically towards managing its expenditure. Typical outcomes from breakthrough thinking might include new product development, business process reengineering, supply-base rationalisation, value engineering, business process outsourcing, supply-chain integration and so on. These are not small-scale incremental changes (such as renegotiating a contract) but should be aimed at delivering large-scale improvement.

It is difficult to quantify these improvements to a single figure, but if cost reduction was the only measure, then a stretching target of at least 20%–25% might be considered. However, as is widely recognised amongst leading experts, category management is far more sophisticated than a one-dimensional focus on cost.

Given the level of challenge in these targets for category management, together with the complexities of a modern-day organisation, Stage 1 (Initiation) represents a critical set of preparation activities for all category management teams. Those who overlook or underplay this initial stage fail to understand how strategic change programmes are successfully delivered in modern organisations. The future strength and sustainability of deliverables rest completely on the rigour that has been applied to this first step.

Put simply, Stage 1 (Initiation) is about setting up and initiating the category review with best-practice project management disciplines. It is about corralling all of the necessary stakeholders across the organisation to focus and agree on a strategic plan of action for a given area of organisational spend. If the category is not given this sense of structure, profile and importance, then it will fail to carry sufficient momentum during the analysis and strategy stages and will be unlikely to deliver meaningful benefits.

Extra explanation and theory

The activities in this stage are about embedding a sense of governance into the management of the category. Some practitioners and consultants will refer to category management as a project, as discussed in this book's introduction. While this isn't strictly true and (wrongly) suggests that category management has an end point (rather than being continuously iterative), this type of thinking can be helpful when setting up and organising a team to review the category, devise a new strategy, implement change and deliver benefits.

One of our clients recently described governance as 'the right people, making the right decisions, at the right time with the right information'. It's a nice summary, but let's not get misled that this is simple.

Governance needs to cover scoping boundaries, accountabilities and decision rights. This requires a competence in managing stakeholders, and the activities within this step are predominantly focused on this essential task. Defining the project team and its wider stakeholder team is critical. Category management is a cross-functional activity designed to bring together the organisation to analyse and agree on the best strategy going forwards. This means that getting the right representation onto the category team is critical.

Many organisations now adopt a three-tiered approach to category team governance, as illustrated in Figure 1.1.

Selecting and co-opting the category sponsor is fundamental. This should be a senior manager at executive/director level in the organisation with the appropriate authority to give the category team the 'mandate' required to operate. Typically this is not a procurement person, especially if an enterprise-wide solution is required. It might be an operations director, the SVP marketing, the CIO/CTO, a chief engineer or any similar senior role that is relevant to the type of spend that's under review.

The sponsor needs to be briefed and co-opted into their role, which will require a commitment of their time to take on a 'figurehead' leadership role and be the chief point of accountability for the category team (similar in many ways to the role of a senior responsible officer in the public sector). This will include regular briefings (typically on a monthly basis) and approvals for the gateway reviews.

Programme managers are only required where there are several categories under review at any one time in an organisation. Principally their role is one of coordination, management, reporting and resourcing. They should not be directly involved in the day-to-day detail of the category team.

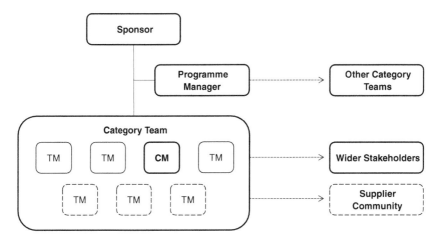

Figure 1.1   Three-tiered governance

If an organisation is engaging consultants to help adopt category management, the programme manager does not need to be from the same consultant company. Any competent and experienced commercial project manager is capable of fulfilling this role.

The category team should therefore comprise a number of team members (TM) or representatives from relevant functional disciplines that are involved with the spend. For example, a category team reviewing packaging expenditure might include the packaging buyer and representatives from production, marketing, logistics and finance. The team would not include anyone from the supply community (i.e. no suppliers), nor anyone else with a conflict of interest.

The category manager (CM) is selected from within the team and his or her management/coordination role is approved by the sponsor. In less mature organisations, category managers are not full-time roles (and neither is the membership of the category team). However, more mature category management often necessitates full-time resource commitment – especially for higher-value and more complex categories.

The level of cross-functional coordination in a category is directly proportional to the amount of value that can be derived from the supply chain, as illustrated in Figure 1.2.

In practice, although practitioners would like to think they can launch a category management initiative and gain 'breakthrough' commercial benefits, the reality is that first-generation category management rarely does. It is often a disjointed response.

The iterative approach to category management takes a longer-term, more strategic view of spend management, recognising that commitment needs to be built up across the organisation before large-scale change can be effected successfully. Only a fully 'integrated' approach to category management will deliver enterprise-wide breakthrough success. Sometimes this only occurs on the second, third or fourth generation (iteration) of category management.

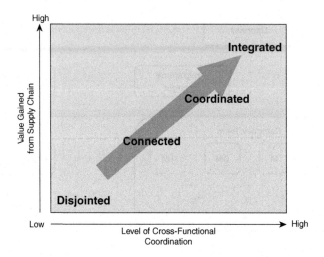

Figure 1.2 Category maturity matrix

Practical hints and tips

1 Take time to select team members who are committed to change and supporters of the category management approach.
2 Teams need to be given time to form and perform. If you need major breakthrough results from a committed team, then consider an appropriate team-building activity.
3 Briefing roles, responsibilities and scope is essential. Everyone needs clarity, both inside and outside the category team.
4 'Mindset' is a key attribute that can unlock value, so it helps to have free thinkers and a 'can-do' attitude in the team. That said, a diverse team usually performs better!
5 Take time to brief the sponsor and gain his or her commitment to the cause.
6 Avoid conflicts of interest and prejudice about the end solution.
7 Be prepared to commit time and resources to the category management approach. The end-to-end process may take an iteration of 8–16 weeks (depending on category complexity, sometimes longer) and Stage 1 can take as long as 6 weeks to set up correctly.
8 Take a project management approach to resourcing and coordinating activities within the category process, even though it's not a project!

Summary of activities

We have detailed seven key activities within this first stage of category management:

1 **Project charter** – This is a simple summary document that defines the scope, resources and objectives of the category review.

2   **Category hierarchy** – This is a classification system that applies across the full organisational spend profile so that the category can be defined and scoped and that all interfaces with other areas of spend are identified.

3   **Team charter** – This summary document identifies the roles, responsibilities and behaviours of the category team to ensure commitment and unity of purpose.

4   **RACI** – This is a summary that charts each of the stakeholders and his or her respective involvement within the category.

5   **Stakeholder management** – This is an approach to identify, classify and subsequently manage each of the internal (or external) stakeholders within a category.

6   **Communication plan** – To support the stakeholder map, this document summarises each of the planned communications to support category activity and progress.

7   **Risk register** – This is an application of best-practice project management disciplines to the category in terms of identifying, assessing, logging and mitigating key risks to delivery on the category.

What the gateway needs to consider

As outlined in the introduction to this handbook, we recommend a specific approval point at the end of each stage that we refer to as a 'gateway'. Ideally this should be treated as a 'go/no-go' gateway, particularly for Stage 1 (Initiation) where the emphasis must be on whether the category governance has been set up appropriately for the ensuing category activities.

Specifically, this needs to ensure that the category review has been appropriately scoped and resourced. It needs to check that project management disciplines have been embedded in the category and the right personnel are on board with a clear vision and understanding of their roles and what activities they need to undertake. On top of this, it is essential that all relevant stakeholders have been identified and, where necessary, engaged about the category activity.

The following checklist gives some more practical guidance on what the category manager should be preparing for the Stage 1 gateway.

Gateway approval checklist

STAGE 1: INITIATION

1 Has the category scope been defined and agreed with all stakeholders? ☐

2 Have stretching/SMART targets been agreed for the category project? ☐

3 Has the category manager been nominated? ☐

4 Has a cross-functional category team been identified and co-opted? ☐

5 Have all stakeholders been identified and initially engaged in the project? ☐

6 Has a category RACI been completed and agreed between all stakeholders? ☐

7 Has the category risk register been created, and have risks and responsibilities been assigned? ☐

8 Has the project charter been established and signed off? ☐

9 Have the project milestone activities and deliverables been agreed and scheduled? ☐

10 Has a comprehensive stakeholder communication plan been developed? ☐

Signed: _____

Category Manager

_____

Sponsor

Activity 1
PROJECT CHARTER

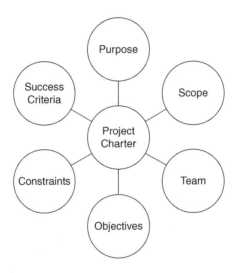

Figure 1.3   Project charter

Overview

The Project Management Institute (PMI) (2017) defines a *project charter* as 'a document issued by senior management that formally authorises the work of the project to begin (or continue) and gives the project manager authority to do his job'. It is regarded as an essential precursor to the planning process and part of the formal initiation of the category process.

Sometimes incorrectly referred to as a 'team charter', the project charter's precise format varies from situation to situation and from team to team. The final approved document formally initiates the project. In effect it is a simpler visual representation of a project initiation document (PID).

The project charter is regarded as an excellent way of clarifying direction and encouraging understanding and buy-in from key stakeholders. It is, in essence, a 'road map' which helps all those involved understand the direction and speed of travel while journeying to the final destination.

Elements

A typical project charter will have the following structure:

Purpose – The reason for initiating the category management process. It can provide a platform for common understanding and vision of what the final delivery might be.

Scope – Identifies what is in scope and what is out of scope. Defining the scope is critical in order to avoid making false assumptions about the project. This will include defining the category of expenditure.

Team – A list of category team members, their roles and time allocations (i.e. full or part time). Some key members may also have their responsibilities defined. This normally relates to the team leader and team sponsor.

Objectives – A clear statement of how the team intends to reach its end goal through a description of the objectives to be achieved. Objectives should be written at a low level so that they can be evaluated at the conclusion of a project to see whether they were achieved or not. A well-worded objective will be SMART (specific, measurable, attainable/achievable, realistic and time bound).

Constraints – This is an opportunity to explore potential issues, roadblocks and risks to category delivery.

Success criteria – A list of criteria that must be met in order to evidence that the category management process has delivered its vision. Some project charters like to develop additional success measures with reference to softer elements such as 'team learning' and 'team dynamics'.

Budget – From time to time category team expenditure may be required (e.g. off-site meetings, team building, visiting reference sites). An estimate of costs will give a fuller picture to those sponsoring the category management, and therefore a reward-versus-effort equation can be made.

Approval process – The appropriate approval process should be ascertained, together with the relevant gateways and associated timings, so that the team can estimate the relevant timings to manage the category, as well as resources and potential key dates.

So what?

By using the project charter as a method of initiation, the category team are following best practice when it comes to 'kicking off' waves of activity. In effect, this formal approach helps establish robust project management procedures to the category management discipline.

The development of a project charter necessitates the early engagement and cooperation of key stakeholders in order to gain consensus and approval, and ergo becomes a useful mechanism for identifying participants' expectations and capturing potential group organisational issues at the start of cross-functional category processes.

Category management application

- Forms a means of formal category project sign-off and approval
- Provides a vision for the category team
- Provides a mechanism for clarifying understanding of team objectives and goals
- Educates others across the business as to the category project's purpose
- Provides an initial estimate of resource allocation that can be made

Limitations

Investing time up front to develop the project charter reduces confusion later on. It enables the team to get it right first time. However, due to increasingly time-pressured working environments, there can be a temptation to complete the document without the support or assistance of the business. Of course, this approach is fundamentally flawed, as one of the main functions of the project charter is to ensure group consensus on ways of working, scope and so forth.

There is also confusion between the discreet roles of the team charter versus the project charter, and either due to misunderstanding or time pressures, these templates are often merged into one, or one or the other is omitted from the category management process.

Furthermore, there is a temptation to treat category management as a discrete project that has a specific end point. While this can be useful for managing various iterations of the category management process, the reality is that category management should be a continuous cycle of activity rather than a discrete project.

Template

The following template can be used to assist with the formation of a category project:

- Template 1: Project charter

Activity 2
CATEGORY HIERARCHY

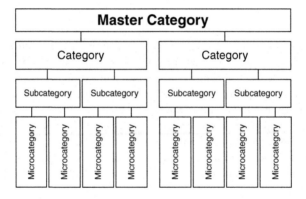

Figure 1.4 Category hierarchy

Overview

The *Oxford English Dictionary* defines a *category* as 'a class or division of people or things regarded as having particular shared characteristics'. Marketers were early pioneers of grouping similarities within categories in order to establish targeted media campaigns to different classes of consumers. Later, the procurement community developed the concept to categorise potential supply-market opportunities and synergies in lieu – with Peter Kraljic being one of the pioneers. Each category and subcategory represented a separate sector within the supply market, thus offering a range of strategic offerings for category managers.

Category hierarchies illustrate how a supply market can be classified and broken down into a number of subgroups for strategic purposes. The classification of these clusters makes it easier for the category manager to understand how to leverage the value effectively from each constituent supply market.

Elements

There are four main classifications of categories. Figure 1.5 outlines each of these, together with an accompanying description and two corresponding examples.

Classification	Description	Example 1	Example 2
Master category	The main grouping from which all other classifications stem; generally, the level at which the master category strategy will be developed.	Facilities management	Information technology (IT)
Category	Identifies groups within the master category with similar characteristics and properties from which individual category strategies could be developed.	Security services	Telecoms
Subcategory	A subgrouping within a category which is used to identify further similarities which may have an impact on the strategy-development process due to the structure of the supply market.	CCTV	Mobile telecoms
Microcategory	An optional subdivision used to identify specific goods or services, such as niche players.	Infrared cameras	Data services

Figure 1.5 Classification of categories

Jean-Philippe Massin (2012) has suggested that there are six factors that organisations should consider when creating categories (which he refers to as 'sourcing groups'): (1) they should be based on a similar supply source, (2) they should possess similar production processes, (3) they should have a similar use or purpose, (4) they should have similar material content, (5) they should have similar specifications and (6) they should employ similar technology. If these six criteria cannot be satisfied, then the reality is that there is a separate category or subcategory that needs to be considered.

Category hierarchies are normally shown in a tree-diagram format, so that the breakdown of category division can be easily seen at a glance. It is recommended that a single 'master' hierarchy is developed for the organisation and that this activity is carried out centrally for the whole of the organisation.

So what?

A category hierarchy helps the team segment goods and services in relation to specific supply-market factors. This means that the resulting category strategy approach should be well placed to deliver the desired business requirements.

Segmenting the goods and services via a structured hierarchical approach will help the team identify possible volume opportunities for suppliers, capacity issues and 'group deal' potential. It should provide a 'big picture' of the overall category strategy for the market.

Having a robust category hierarchy gives the organisation a clear 'road map' for which categories to address. It acts as a scoping tool and helps prevent duplication between category teams. Effective hierarchies should provide category teams with strategic options to aggregate or disaggregate subcategories. Effective hierarchies should also help identify synergies between related categories and highlight the various interdependencies between expenditure.

Category management application

- Provides a classification system that helps structure categories in relation to the supply market
- Allows for categories/subcategories and associated responsibilities to be delegated to team members
- Allows for category/subcategory 'waves'/'phases' to be scheduled into the category management plan
- Assists with opportunity/leverage identification

Limitations

The categorisation process can become unwieldy, and so there needs to be clear boundaries around the scope of 'what's in' and 'what's out' of each category. There can also be a lot of crossover amongst products, and so care needs to be taken to avoid duplication of effort, resources and strategy during the category-planning phase.

One of the category manager's biggest challenges is to get accurate and meaningful spend data to match each of the categories and subcategories. This is one of the current 'blights' of enterprise-wide spend data. Essentially the classification system that sits behind these systems (often referred to as a 'material group coding') needs to be rewritten around the category hierarchy in order for the spend data to provide the most value. If this is not aligned, then the category manager's effectiveness is severely hampered despite the appeal of these 'big data' systems.

Ultimately, analysing categories in detail is seen as a useful part of the category management process, but the hierarchy approach can be viewed as 'overkill' in some instances, where, for example, the need to go down to the microlevel just isn't viable or necessary. It should also be noted that some organisations prefer to develop individual category plans without first developing the category hierarchy, unfortunately seeing the latter as surplus to requirements.

Template

The following template can be used to identify category clusters:

- Template 2: Category hierarchy

Activity 3
TEAM CHARTER

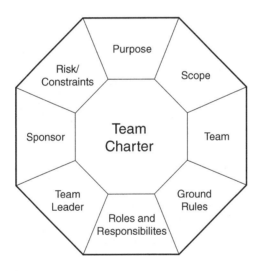

Figure 1.6 Team charter

Overview

The team charter is viewed as an ancillary document to the project charter. Its primary focus is the team – how it communicates, behaves and performs – together with detail around roles and responsibilities. It is designed to be completed in a team environment with core members.

In keeping with the project charter, its completion should be carried out at the earliest opportunity, as it will engender support and buy-in from cross-functional participants. It allows those representatives from the business to have a say in how team meetings should be run (e.g. meeting etiquette, conflict-resolution procedure) and away-day budgets.

The team charter may be populated once the project charter has been formally approved.

Elements

The intent of a team charter is to create an understanding of how the core team will function and its accompanying dynamics. It is viewed as providing extra granularity to the 'team' element of a project charter. A typical team charter will have the following structure:

Purpose – The reason for creating the cross-functional category team is restated from the project charter. This ensures consistency in terms of a common understanding and vision of what the final delivery may be.

Scope – The scope is also repeated from the project charter. This supports a continual awareness of the team's boundaries. It may be that, at this stage, some members can give even more definition to this element.

Team – This is a list of core category team members, their roles and time allocations (i.e. full or part time). This section may also identify additional resources and stakeholder groups that could be useful to the cause.

Ground rules – In general these refer to expectations relating to behaviour and can include a list of what is deemed acceptable and unacceptable, values and conflict-resolution processes.

Member roles and responsibilities – Team member roles and responsibilities are described within this section. For example, the team member representing the marketing function may be allocated a communication role and his or her responsibilities will include promoting the category project across the organisation and originating e-mail editorial opportunities.

Team leader responsibilities – This role is seen as critical to the success of the project. Discussing the responsibilities of the leader within the team environment will facilitate clarity and endorsement of the position.

Sponsor responsibilities – Very often team sponsors are not present at group meetings, as they are lending support through their seniority rather than through active participation. In essence, they become a route for coalition building and escalation. However, their level of involvement will still need to be agreed and documented within the team charter.

Risks/constraints – This is an opportunity to identify risks to the success of the team and potential organisational and political barriers.

So what?

The team charter furnishes the project charter with another layer of detail relating to the operation of the category team. It serves as a source of information for members to illustrate the structure, workings and direction of the team, as well as educate others across the organisation. It is a 'living' document, and therefore should be constantly updated upon team movement.

It is important that a team charter is discussed in detail as a group during the early stages of a category project. Putting in the required time to develop the template can act as an important 'binding agent' for those participating, while reducing the risk of conflict and tension. Early consensus will establish parameters and guidelines for behaviour from the outset. This will also help a team mature quickly and pass through the inevitable 'storming' stage of early team development (Tuckman, 1965).

Category management application

- Assists the category team development process
- Provides guidelines for team behaviour
- Clarifies and endorses the category team lead role
- Defines in detail core team member roles and responsibilities
- Facilitates commitment to the team

Limitations

As previously stated under Activity 1, there is some confusion surrounding the difference between the team charter and project charter. This often leads to one or the other of these being omitted from the category management process. Frequently, this tends to be the team version, as it is not deemed as necessary or important, and the content can be regarded as 'fluffy'.

There also appears to be uncertainty as to who should lead the completion of the charter. Academics argue that this should be carried out by the appointed team sponsor; however, in practice, it is more likely to be the team leader who performs this function. Finally, the team charter, if completed properly, can be a time-consuming process, and many teams fail to put aside the requisite time or resource to achieve the end result.

Worse still, time restrictions can influence team leaders to preplan the input in advance, which of course goes against the spirit and intent of this document.

Template

The following template can be used to clarify category team roles and responsibilities:

- Template 3: Team charter

Activity 4
RACI

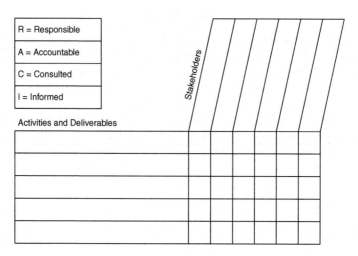

| R = Responsible |
| A = Accountable |
| C = Consulted |
| I = Informed |

Activities and Deliverables

Figure 1.7 RACI

Overview

A RACI chart is a form of a responsibility assignment matrix, commonly referred to as a RAM. RACI is an acronym that derives its name from the four variables – responsible, accountable, consulted and informed – which are applied to participants in the project so that there is a common understanding of roles and responsibilities across the team.

The RACI can be confused (wrongly) with the RAQSCI model, and although both are popular project management tools, each has an entirely different focus (see Stage 2, Activity 8). There are many adaptations of the RACI, such as RACISO (responsible, accountable, consulted, informed, stakeholder, ownership) and PACSI (problem, accountable, consulted, stakeholder, informed). The template format can vary significantly depending upon the complexity and needs of the project.

Elements

The RACI chart is normally in tabular format and depicts each individual associated with the project, together with their RACI status in relation to their assigned roles for a given task. Each variable is explained as follows:

Responsible – Those who have been assigned responsibility for delivering a task. There is always at least one individual who will be attributed this role, and others can also be delegated tasks in order to support him or her.

Accountable – Those individuals ultimately answerable for the completion of the task/deliverable. Accountability is sometimes delegated to others, but it is considered best practice to avoid sharing accountability between individuals. The individual who is accountable must approve work that others have been delegated responsibility for.

Consulted – Those individuals and key stakeholders that must be consulted with as part of the project, for example senior managers not directly involved but who have organisational power and are interested in the overall direction and success of the team, or subject-matter experts who have a vital part to play in terms of product specification. Typically, this is a two-way communication process.

Informed – Those individuals or stakeholders least involved with the project. They just need to be kept up to date with progression and next steps. Typically, this is a one-way communication process.

It should be noted that a 'role' is a descriptor of an associated set of tasks, which may be performed by any number of people, and conversely one person can perform many roles. For example, a category project team may have five people who can undertake the role of category lead, although practically there will only be one, while an individual who is able to perform the role of category lead may also be able to take on other roles within the project, such as communication lead.

So what?

RACI is a way of mapping out 'who does what' in relation to a category project. The aim is for every task to be assigned responsible and accountable roles. The chart should then be discussed amongst team members in order to ensure there is a general consensus of approach, which in turn avoids duplication of effort and the potential development of conflict.

RACI's main strength is in the way in which it can improve communication within a team. If used correctly, not only do all participants understand with whom and how they should be communicating, but it also could also reduce the amount of e-mail traffic (i.e. by providing distinction between those who should be consulted versus those who should be informed only). Thus, overall the team will evolve to be more cooperative, aligned and productive.

Category management application

- Provides a technique for creating alignment within the team
- Avoids duplication of effort and potential conflict in relation to communication
- Clearly identifies accountability and responsibility
- Serves as a governance document within the team

Limitations

The RACI is frequently incorrectly used as a stakeholder management tool and not as a RAM. Such application has flaws, since the RACI does not assess the relationship of the stakeholder to the project. For this to occur, an additional framework would need to be considered, such as Mendelow's power/interest matrix (see Activity 5).

The RACI chart can also be seen as a complicated process for smaller organisations to take on board, and some authors in the field of procurement criticise it for being 'overengineered'. In essence, it is a tool designed for managing projects with a high level of complexity or a large number of stakeholders, rather than a category management tool per se. This may be contrary to the views of some consulting firms, who see benefit in additional layers of project management tools for each and every category project, thus removing potential 'agility' and pace from category planning.

Finally, it should be noted that RACI charts are not dynamic in nature and, therefore, need constant updating as the wider organisational environment changes over time.

Template

The following template may be used to assess individual accountability and responsibility within a category team:

- Template 4: RACI chart

Activity 5
STAKEHOLDER
MANAGEMENT

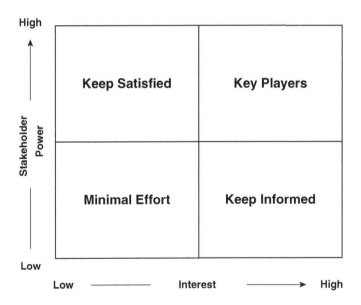

Figure 1.8 The power/interest matrix

Source: adapted from Mendelow (1991)

Overview

First published in 1991, this model looks at understanding the influence that different stakeholders have on category development. It does this by classifying the stakeholders in relation to the power they hold and the extent to which they are likely to show an interest in supporting or opposing the project accordingly.

Elements

Although the power of each stakeholder will vary from industry to industry, market to market and country to country, two key factors will remain the same:

- the interest each stakeholder shows in communicating his or her expectations on the organisation's category management strategy;
- the levels of power and persuasion the stakeholder possesses to enable this to occur.

The four key elements of the matrix are as follows:

1 **Low power / low interest** – The stakeholders in this group do not require much effort in consultation.
2 **Low power / high interest** – These stakeholders need to be kept informed, but mostly as a matter of courtesy, since they have little power.
3 **Low interest / high power** – These stakeholders need to be kept satisfied because they have high power and they could prove resistant if they were to be upset by category team actions.
4 **High interest / high power** – These are the 'key players' who must be consulted and considered at every stage of the category project because their active support is needed to get things done. They are likely to have direct influence on and responsibility for resources that are needed.

So what?

Understanding stakeholders in this way can enable better and more meaningful communication. For example, continually arranging face-to-face meetings with a stakeholder who has little power could be avoided and thus more focus placed on those that are key decision makers.

This model can be extended beyond just category management to be applied to any aspect of supply-chain delivery.

Category management application

- Builds a profile of key business stakeholders in the category management project
- Assists with building cross-functional relationships
- Helps gain support and buy-in to category management decision making
- Identifies areas of potential conflict (organisation vs. stakeholder and stakeholder vs. stakeholder)

Limitations

This matrix provides a simple way of analysing stakeholders; however, once this activity has been performed, it does not aid in understanding how to appropriately communicate with stakeholders. For this, the work of Richard Daft and Robert Lengel (1998) is recommended.

Template

The following template can be used to assess key stakeholders in a category project:

*   Template 5: Stakeholder management matrix

Activity 6
COMMUNICATION PLAN

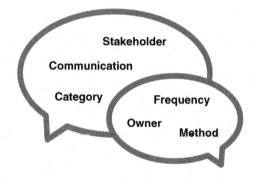

Figure 1.9 Communications planning

Overview

A communication plan is a popular way of developing a schedule of proactive communications for a category project. It formally defines who should be given specific information, when it should be delivered and what communication channels should be used to convey key messages. The plan may also be the repository of the category project glossary and approved channel templates, such as 'team briefs' and 'executive reports'.

It should be noted that the term 'communication plan' can be confused with 'communications planning', which is an integral part of the marketing communications process rather than category management.

Elements

The communication plan should capture all intended written, spoken and electronic interaction across the category team and its stakeholders, addressing the following:

- assessment of the information and its flow in and out of the category project;
- identification of the recipients of the information;
- decisions on time frames for information release;
- agreement on the format of the information;
- allocation of responsibility for transmitting and providing the information.

The key elements of a communication plan will classically revolve around these main areas:

Stakeholder – Individuals who need to be aware of the communication. These should be subdivided between those that are internal and those that are external to the organisation.

Category – This is the category or subcategory which the communication relates to or affects.

Communication – This is the message content that needs to be communicated (e.g. progress, risks, milestones, meetings).

Method – This details the way in which the message will be communicated (e.g. project status reports, face-to-face briefings, minutes, conference calls, blogs, social media, etc.).

Frequency – This denotes how often the message needs to be communicated (e.g. one-off, monthly, weekly, etc.).

Owner – These are the individuals delegated with the responsibility for ensuring that the communication is activated.

Completion date – This is the date by which the communication will have taken place.

So what?

Developing a communication plan is a systematic way of ensuring that key messaging surrounding a category project is handled appropriately. Depending upon the size and complexity of the category project, it may be that a team member is dedicated solely to undertaking this task.

There are many communication frameworks which can assist with the building of a successful plan. A popular methodology is PACE, an acronym which stands for primary, alternate, contingency and emergency; it is often used to help project team members understand the most fitting communication channels internally. For example, the primary mode of communication could be web based or e-mail, alternate could be landline telephone, contingency could be via mobile, while emergency could be face to face. The mode selected will be dependent upon the information technology available and culture of the organisation.

Category management application

- Provides a recognised way of managing and controlling project communication
- Provides a disciplined project management approach

- Is a mechanism for allocating ownership of messaging
- Helps identify suitable ways of interacting across the organisation
- Protects against last-minute/'seat-of-the-pants' miscommunication

Limitations

A communication plan is viewed as best practice when it comes to the dissemination of project information, and there are very few limitations to speak of, other than the size and flexibility of the document. For instance, it should be capable of expansion should the project scope need to increase; however the range of headings within the plan should be contained to those suggested, as the purpose of it can become confused with other category documents, such as RACI and the risk register.

It should also be noted that poorly constructed communication plans can lead to more questions than they answer, especially where a 'one size fits all' approach is instituted, which can mean that many stakeholders are copied in to updates that they needn't be, which can become frustrating to those involved and lead to inefficiency and ineffectiveness from a communications perspective.

One of the biggest risks associated with communications planning is the assumption that all recipients will want to receive the message. Category managers should consider a variety of methods and include innovative communication methods (e.g. setting up project blogs or bespoke social media sites). It must also be remembered that effective communication is two way. Category management requires cross-functional engagement, and so consultations also need to be built into the communication plan.

Template

The following template can be used to support communication mapping:

- Template 6: Communication plan

Activity 7
RISK REGISTER

Figure 1.10 The risk management cycle

Overview

A risk register or risk log is a common tool used within project management. It is used to record and manage all risks, actions and responsibilities in relation to a category project or programme. It is applied within category management as a way of understanding on a daily basis the potential likelihood and impact of each risk and ergo how it might be controlled or mitigated.

There are numerous formats available. The document may be either qualitative or quantitative, dependent upon the ranking method used; for example a qualitative approach may assess risk as either 'high', 'medium' or 'low', while a quantitative system will view risk more numerically, such as with probability percentages. It is possible to mix qualitative with quantitative assessment, although care must be taken in doing so, in order to ensure standardisation of the various analyses.

Elements

To establish a risk register, a facilitated workshop is considered best practice. This way, all category team members and wider stakeholders can assist in the identification of risks that may be associated with a particular category management programme and consequently could have an impact on cost, time or performance. Where possible, information from the team should also be obtained on the impact of the risk and the likelihood of its occurrence.

Once developed, the risk register should be made available to all category team members to actively encourage reporting and resolution activity. Ideally only a small number of individuals should be responsible for managing and updating the document itself. This ensures that an accurate tracking approach to risk is undertaken.

There are many variations and examples of risk registers. The majority contain the following elements at a minimum:

Identification of risks – A short name or number to identify the risk quickly.
Ranking – A priority list which is determined by the relative ranking of the risks.
Status – A report on the current standing of the risk (i.e. whether the risk is increasing, decreasing, static, under review or dead).
Description – A fuller description of the risk which should cover the main characteristics (e.g. how it is likely to proceed in terms of pace and severity).
Metrics – Information relating to potential impact, probability and proximity.
Responsibility – Named individuals attached to ownership/accountability, delegated responsibility and rectification.
Mitigation action – The actions that need to take place in order to control the risk.
Completion date – The date by which the mitigating action will have taken place.

Risk registers should be version controlled and reviewed on a regular basis if they are to be effective.

So what?

A structured approach to risk assessment can highlight areas of potential danger at an early stage in the category management process. This not only supports mitigation but also assigns visible ownership, placing pressure on those responsible to carry out the necessary activity as soon as it is practicable or at the very latest by the stated completion date in the risk register/log.

While it is important to involve as many stakeholders in the risk assessment process as possible, some category management authors also advocate that suppliers be involved, but this will clearly need to be based on the relevancy and maturity of the relationship.

Category management application

- Establishes a group consensus of potential programme risks
- Identifies and describes risks associated with the category management process

- Provides a mechanism for managing risks via allocation of ownership
- Fends off potential issues at an early stage

Limitations

Risk registers/logs are used not only within project scenarios but also within organisations more generally. They are widely acknowledged as a positive influence within the working environment; however, research has found that they can in some instances lead to an 'illusion of control', which can result in complacency and risks not being dealt with adequately.

There has also been much academic research and accompanying criticism in relation to the effort required to manage and administer the risk register – the main thrust of the argument being that it can become 'an industry' tying up many valuable resources. This appears to be especially true of organisations with a risk-averse culture.

It should be remembered that risk registers demand constant review, and unless a rigorous monitoring process is undertaken on a regular basis, the document can become nonfunctional with out-of-date information, which in turn may divert focus away from critical areas.

Template

The following template can be used to assess risks that may occur during a category project:

- Template 7: Risk register

STAGE 2

Research

Overview and benefits of this stage

Successful category management is underpinned by robust data and rigorous analysis. To create and implement a strategy, you need to have a thorough insight into all of the relevant information, characteristics and trends that apply, both internally (in terms of organisational behaviour and spend patterns) and externally (in terms of market dynamics).

This is a time-consuming and potentially resource-intensive stage in the category management process. Good strategy is based on good knowledge, and so the temptations of shortcuts here need to be resisted. This is category management's equivalent of big data.

It's impossible to give guidance on the timeline for the research phase of category management. You need 'enough' time to gather all of the internal and external data required to make a full analysis of the category – and that depends on how big an impact you want to make, how much you really know about the category and how far you are willing to search for potential breakthrough solutions.

As a guideline, we think this stage requires at least 40% of the overall project timeline as a rough 'rule of thumb' – but this is very approximate. We have worked with some companies that believe this can be completed in just one or two weeks, and others that have taken some three to six months researching their category.

A well-organised 'mature' organisation with a strategic and well-developed approach to category management will assume a knowledge management approach to category management. They know that this research phase represents an 'investment' in future value breakthroughs – not just for the first iteration, but for subsequent category management cycles too.

In other words, as long as you store the data you gather from your first attempts at researching a category, you can use this again and build on it in future iterations (i.e. the investment in time and resources will not be as much when you review the category strategy in the future). The only caveat is that all historic data need

29

to be checked and updated if they are to be relied on. It is therefore worth your category team thinking through how they will store, maintain and version control the output as they progress through this category management stage.

Conversely, organisations that take a half-hearted approach to researching their categories tend to achieve suboptimal results and later dismiss category management for failing to deliver sufficient value.

Extra explanation and theory

Research can be time-consuming and costly on resources. More recently there has been a growing trend to rely on market data supplied by third-party consultancies. There are significant risks with this approach! The gain in expediency (you get the research output quicker) is a significant compromise on the quality of the insight gained.

To understand this point, we have to go back to review why you are undertaking the research in the first place. The purpose of researching the category is to ensure that a full analysis can be undertaken to achieve deep understanding of the category. In other words, undertaking research is part of the learning process; it helps category teams discover the underlying characteristics, trends and issues. As the category team explores this, aside of learning more, it also starts to gain initial ideas about potential options for solutions. Researching the detail of the category helps the category team understand and analyse the current and future situations – and this insight is essential to the longer-term success of the category management initiative.

It is understandable why some organisations outsource data gathering to third parties. They sell a good story about being 'experts' and having the right resources, and they can affect a quick turnaround. For organisations lacking the right resources, this is appealing. Ultimately this is a mini 'make/buy' decision about an element of category management but, before jumping to conclusions, think of the risks of sub-optimising the outputs. While the power of the Internet and global sources of data is strong, is it really possible that a team of analysts halfway round the world in a different economy is really going to offer valuable knowledge and insight into your specific market? Understanding the nuances between a global market and more localised regional, national or local markets is unlikely to be understood in full from a distance.

There are two main areas of data that need to be researched, illustrated in Figure 2.1.

Internal research data	External research data
Changing business requirements	Product (and service) details
Functional requirements	Nature of supply markets (global, regional, national and local)
Stakeholders	Competitors and other buyers
Buying behaviour (timing, seasonality)	Supply-chain variables
Spend patterns (historic and current)	Technical, legislative and environmental standards

Figure 2.1   Internal and external research

Internal research data	External research data
Fragmentation/aggregation	Consumer behaviour
Future demand profiles	Prices, costs and 'should cost'
Ordering procedures and so forth	Key suppliers and so forth

Figure 2.1 Continued

One of the most fundamental pieces of research is understanding the current and future 'business requirements'. You will see that this gets an activity of its own in this stage.

Understanding and mapping the business requirements is the starting point in getting stakeholders to commit to paper their hopes and expectations for any given spend. From here the business requirements are refined into a set of functional (and then technical) criteria, which becomes the basis for the contract specifications, key performance indicators and contract award criteria – so it's important to invest time getting this right (and not to assume that your supplier will be able to second-guess what you really wanted later on).

The practical challenges of this are never as easy as the theory suggests. Stakeholders often disagree on business requirements, and so the category manager must facilitate a discussion and agreement (possibly a compromise) on the nature and priority of business requirements. We refer to this as establishing a 'hierarchy of needs' in much the same philosophy as Maslow. An example is shown in Figure 2.2.

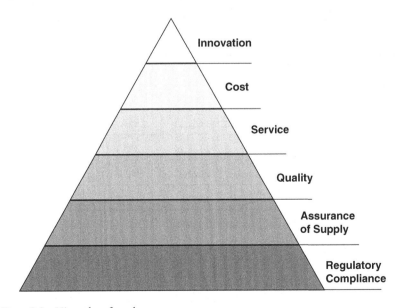

Figure 2.2 Hierarchy of needs

This example helps demonstrate the priority ranking of different functional requirements, with the basic needs at the base of the hierarchy and more desirable features above. This kind of prioritisation approach is far more useful to the category team than a stakeholder who simply says, 'I want it all', and it allows a deeper understanding of what trade-offs might be acceptable as a solution. Remember, the priority ranking will differ between individual categories of spend.

Another area of challenge when undertaking internal analysis is that of internal spend analysis. It remains one of the biggest areas of weakness amongst most organisations; the value of spend data is only as good as the care with which it has been captured.

Take for example the spend analysis that came from one of our clients (a public-sector municipality) in Figure 2.3.

Category spend data (Level 1)	Spend ($)	% of spend	No. of vendors
Environmental services	49,974,209.20	32.60	74
Construction	17,834,550.65	11.63	231
Facilities management services	12,912,034.01	8.42	142
HR services	11,003,769.17	7.18	23
IT and telecoms	8,793,155.93	5.74	112
Unclassified	7,503,112.79	4.89	1,932
Utilities	6,782,046.88	4.42	35
Consultancy	6,340,848.12	4.14	172
Social care (adults and children)	5,855,841.77	3.82	22
Construction materials	3,979,399.20	2.60	324
Horticultural	3,713,661.33	2.42	796
Other	3,272,556.14	2.13	7,803
Vehicle management	2,914,022.03	1.90	55
Arts and leisure	2,750,000.00	1.79	3
Financial services	1,914,338.73	1.25	34
Education	1,300,498.47	0.85	56
Catering	1,145,294.44	0.75	309

Figure 2.3 Example spend analysis

Category spend data (Level 1)	Spend ($)	% of spend	No. of vendors
Sports and playground equipment	873,487.94	0.57	17
Mail services	767,486.73	0.50	4
Clothing	673,489.99	0.44	75
Cleaning services	671,328.57	0.44	268
Office consumables	597,812.88	0.39	56
Transportation	485,339.36	0.32	7
Healthcare	288,433.26	0.19	9
Stationery	256,423.79	0.17	43
Health and safety	188,923.45	0.12	34
Street and traffic management	126,743.78	0.08	5
Highway equipment and materials	96,755.05	0.06	6
Domestic products	50,343.10	0.03	7
Grand total	$153,289,382.70	100%	12,655

Figure 2.3 Continued

The table shows how the annual third-party spend has been captured across a year at an initial (Level 1) categorisation. Further detail beneath each spend line revealed a more detailed analysis of spend at Levels 2 and 3.

While initially looking useful (and a lot of public money was spent setting up this system and subsequently populating it), it is more or less useless in its current form. The definitions of each of the spend lines are far too broad and ambiguous. Their meaning and scope is open to interpretation and so general users across the organisation are unable to classify spend on a day-to-day basis with any accuracy. Many coding lines have interchangeable meaning and there are also 'dump' codes, such as 'other' and 'unclassified' (7.02% of the total spend). This makes meaningful analysis almost impossible without a drop-down analysis to individual invoices, which would be extremely resource intensive and slow. It's a case of 'rubbish in, rubbish out', where this example has not been designed intelligently.

Unfortunately, this remains a common problem across many large organisations today. We refer back to the chapter on category hierarchy (Stage 1, Activity 2) and suggest that spend-data systems need to capture and classify data around the definitions of categories and subcategories if they are to be productive when analysing and developing an effective category strategy later in the process.

Practical hints and tips

1 Be clear about what data you need to gather (and why) before you start.
2 Prioritise data gathering around what's most important, rather than which is easiest to gather.
3 Use a templated approach to help guide and inform you.
4 Proactively use the category team and wider stakeholders, and involve them in the data sorting and synthesising processes.
5 Take an iterative approach to research with allocation of roles for ownership and so forth.
6 Apply a knowledge management approach to storage, accessibility, security, updating and version control.
7 Be wary of research companies that will 'do it all' for you.
8 Avoid 'analysis paralysis', and remember that category management is an ongoing iterative process.

Summary of activities

We have highlighted seven key activities outlined within this stage of the category management process:

1 **Business requirements (RAQSCI)** – This is a fundamental consultation process to identify the base functional requirements of the spend and their respective priority.
2 **Category profile** – This templated approach is used to create a summary outline of the category and its characteristics, features and trends which then becomes the basis of analysis and subsequent strategy.
3 **Data gathering** – This is the process of structured and proactive data gathering to support the research and analysis of a category.
4 **Key supplier profile** – This profiling tool is used to gather information on each of the 'key players' amongst the supply base. This is not a shortlisting process, but just an opportunity to research and learn about some of the more influential suppliers.
5 **Day one analysis** – This initial analytical tool is used to obtain an early indication of the potential strategy that could be considered for a category of spend.
6 **Situational analysis (STP)** – This is a very simple but effective summarising and problem-defining tool for category managers to use at different stages of the category management process.
7 **Purchase-price cost analysis (PPCA)** – This is a rigorous, detailed and structured approach to cost breakdown, analysis and development of the 'should cost' for individual products and services within a category.

What the gateway needs to consider

The temptation for category management practitioners to create a shortcut through this stage and to bypass a methodical and structured approach to research is very high. If this happens, there is a risk that any analysis and strategy is based on unfounded assumptions, which could in turn jeopardise the value of the outputs from the category management initiative.

We recommend that a specific approval point (gateway) is considered at the end of Stage 2 (Research) where the emphasis must be on whether the category research and the data gathered are sufficiently robust for detailed analysis and strategising to commence. The inclusion of a 'go/no-go' decision helps control the category team and ensure that focus is given to robust data gathering.

The following checklist gives some more practical guidance on what the category manager should be preparing for the Stage 2 gateway.

Gateway approval checklist

STAGE 2: RESEARCH

1 Have the business requirements for the category been identified and prioritised? ☐

2 Has all historic, current and projected spend been identified and analysed for this category? ☐

3 Have all existing preferred (and nonpreferred) suppliers been identified? ☐

4 Have all relevant existing supply contracts and specifications been collated and reviewed? ☐

5 Have current supplier prices been analysed and an appropriate level of cost breakdown established? ☐

6 Have all the relevant internal and external data been gathered, and has a category profile created? ☐

7 Has a key supplier profile been created for any major/influential suppliers in the category? ☐

8 Has a risk register and project plan been reviewed and updated? ☐

9 Has an initial situational analysis been carried out using STP? ☐

10 Have all the relevant stakeholders been consulted on the outputs of this stage of the category management process? ☐

Signed: _____

Category Manager

_____

Sponsor

Activity 8
BUSINESS REQUIREMENTS (RAQSCI)

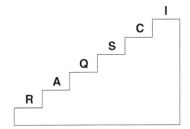

Figure 2.4   Business requirements

Overview

The RAQSCI framework, based on the 'staircase' principle, allows a hierarchical analysis of business requirements to be undertaken. There are many similarly named techniques, such as AQSCIR, AQSCI or the project management model RACI. The latter, while sounding almost identical, is applied in the context of defining roles and responsibilities, rather than defining business needs, and so the two should not be confused when embarking upon the planning process.

The order of the RAQSCI hierarchy is central to the success of the analysis task. Each step in the staircase represents a potential business requirement which must be fully identified and scoped before commencing the next stage.

Elements

Each stage in the RAQSCI process builds upon the ones preceding it. The category manager should ensure that both the internal and external environments have been assessed in order to complete the review. What RAQSCI stands for is illustrated in Figure 2.5.

Business	Description	Example
Regulatory	Complies with identified legislation.	Must comply with health and safety legislation.
Availability	Continuing availability of product. A range of factors may need to be considered, such as supply-chain risk and vulnerability, CSR and the supplier's financial stability.	Must have sufficient production capacity to ensure on-time deliveries.
Quality	Consistency and fitness for purpose of the product.	Must be ISO 9001 accredited.
Service	Factors associated with the service element of the product (i.e. account management structure, training and after-sales support).	Must have a help desk available from 09:00 to 17:00, Monday to Friday.
Cost	All aspects of cost and price.	Must hold prices for a period of four years.
Innovation	Continually improving the product (i.e. creating competitive advantage, developing additional value).	Must have processes in place to encourage idea generation and technical adaption of product.

Figure 2.5 Business requirements explained

So what?

Understanding business requirements is an integral part of category management and will influence the eventual sourcing process in terms of route to the supply market, evaluation criteria and negotiation strategy. Additionally, it provides the platform for contract and supplier relationship–management metrics through the identification of appropriate key performance indicators.

The process for defining business requirements cannot come from procurement alone, and key stakeholders will have to be involved at an early stage in order to inform, secure buy-in and overcome any conflicting concerns and perspectives. The RAQSCI stepping sequence is arranged in such a way so that the issue of 'cost' does not become the initial focus of discussion between procurement and stakeholders, and thus other variables such as quality and service can be fully scoped without placing a cap on price.

Agreeing a consolidated list of needs can often take several rounds of internal debate so that the main ones can be identified. These will then drive the resulting category plan, which should support business strategy and objectives, while also aligning with the overall vision for the organisation.

Category management application

- Provides a structured approach to agreeing priorities and a mechanism for dialogue and debate
- Provides a technique for creating alignment with stakeholder requirements
- Engages and enlists key stakeholder support
- Develops a hierarchy of business needs
- Provides critical input into the category plan and a catalyst for other forms of analysis

Limitations

RAQSCI is popular analysis tool, and the staircase approach allows the category manager to engage in meaningful dialogue with key stakeholders in a structured way. However, the model is often misused, as the hierarchy is ignored, and other variables such as cost are presented as primary factors. Another issue with the hierarchy mechanism would appear to be that, in practice, business needs at each stage are not fully scoped before moving onto the next stage, and so conflict can ensue.

There has also been criticism in relation to 'what's missing', and that the RAQSCI framework is aimed at manufacturing environments rather than services and therefore does not take into account softer business needs such as 'cultural fit' and' relationship dynamics', or, for example, as in the case of the public sector, 'community benefits'.

Finally, it should be remembered that RAQSCI can be 'held hostage' by the loudest voice around the table, or when procurement team input is viewed as transactional rather than strategic.

Template

The following template can be used to prioritise business requirements:

- Template 8: RAQSCI

Activity 9
CATEGORY PROFILE

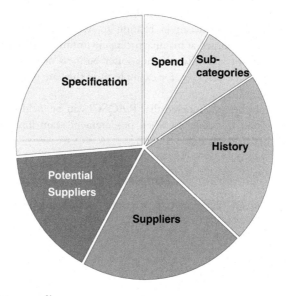

Figure 2.6 Category profile

Overview

Creating a category profile requires in-depth research of the organisational expenditure that is incorporated within in each category. This information is normally developed as a precursor to the supply-market profile, as it helps the category team define all of the key internal information relating to the category, such as scope, business requirements, spend patterns, and contracts and so forth. The collation of relevant data is systematically gathered through a template approach, which sets out the internal detail needed to assist with the development of a category strategy.

External data are assembled later on using the supply-market profile and supplier profile guides.

Elements

There are several areas of intelligence that need to be gathered in relation to the category. Figure 2.7 lists each main informational section and potential subsections together with accompanying examples.

Section	Potential subsection(s)	Examples
Organisational spend patterns	• Spend by site/business unit • Spend by cost centre • Spend by budget	Budgeted expenditure – $3m per year
Category spend	• Spend by segmented category • Forecasted volumes of spend	Segmented spend: Master category – $3m; Category 1 – $1m; Category 2 – $1m; Subcategory – $1m.
Price history	• Unit price • Price history • Price drivers • Unit price per user (if not one single price across organisation)	Three price increases in the last two years. Supply capacity issues driving price up.
Supplier base within organisation	• Number of suppliers used • Spend by supplier • Top three suppliers per category/subcategory/microcategory • Supplier Pareto analysis (80/20)	Five suppliers used across the organisation. 80% of Category 1 spend with one supplier.
Existing contract commitments	• Contract durations • Volume commitments • Notice period • Termination provisions • Any other restrictions	All contracts have six months to run, with a three-month notice period of termination.
Category specification	• Number of specifications being used • Rationalisation undertaken • Specification synergies	Four different specifications for Category 1 being used across the organisation.
Additional considerations	• Compliance to standards • Compliance to regulations • Specific customer requirements • Organisational boundaries	Specifications must comply with ISO 9001.

Figure 2.7   Elements of category profile

So what?

A deeper understanding of how a category is bought, managed and consumed across a business will help drive a more effective category strategy. An internal focus means that key stakeholders, users and functions can be identified in order to gauge business-wide coverage.

A few category management processes compare the category profiling analysis with current business requirements using RAQSCI, which supports the assessment of potential specification gaps; however, this is not a common practice.

A comprehensive category profile that captures all organisational expenditure may enable rationalisation of specifications, suppliers and contracts, thus enhancing the ability to negotiate volume-related pricing or any other value-for-money opportunities that become apparent.

Category management application

- Supports the development of the category strategy
- Complements supply-market profiling
- Provides a foundation for an initial evaluation of potential category strategies
- Assists in identifying opportunities for supply-market leverage and added value

Limitations

There is general agreement across authors and practitioners alike that completion of the category profile is a worthwhile and useful activity to undertake during the category management process, even if collating the input data can be time-consuming.

However, there is often confusion between this activity and the supply-market profile template (which focuses on the collation of external category-related data). Some organisations combine the two in order to decrease the amount of 'template filling' and argue that it is difficult not to include the external supply market when completing a review of a product.

Template

The following template can be used to gather internal data relating to the category:

- Template 9: Category profile

Activity 10
DATA GATHERING

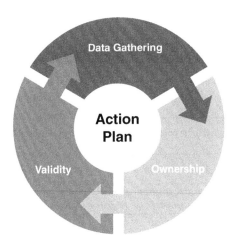

Figure 2.8   Data gathering

Overview

Data gathering is an essential part of category analysis and strategy development. The data-gathering action plan can facilitate the collection of category information, such as the number of players in a market and the supply-market dynamics. The data can be either qualitative or quantitative, but crucially data must be accurate and robust.

Data-gathering action plans can be developed in consultation with the category team or in isolation. Best practice supports a team approach, as it is thought that specialist knowledge held by individual members is more easily identified and accessed, leading to more efficient use of available project resources.

Elements

The idea of establishing a plan around data-gathering activities is to ensure that ownership is ascribed and therefore accompanying action will result.

Data can be derived from a plethora of sources and may be classified as either primary or secondary in the first instance. Primary data refers to that which are researched and sourced directly by the user, such as an interview with a supplier, as opposed to secondary data, which are obtained indirectly through third-party sources, such as magazines, published indices and so on. The data can be further subdivided into qualitative or quantitative and so on.

It should be remembered that there is a difference between data and information, and so further analysis and interpretation is often required to help make the data useful. A typical data-gathering action plan would pose a number of searching questions as outlined in Figure 2.9 (in which a corresponding example is also given).

Data collection questions	Example
Who will collect the data?	Team members as agreed
What data need to be collected to support the project?	Supply market, pricing trends, competition analysis
Where do the data need to be collected from (source)?	Suppliers, desk research, intranet, industry magazines
What is the frequency of data collection?	Industry magazines reviewed monthly for new stories and features
Who are the sampling/focus groups?	Interview with stakeholder focus group
Data collection questions	Example
How will the data be analysed?	Quantitative data to be analysed using Excel, qualitative data to be reviewed by team
How will the data be represented?	Quantitative data to be in the form of bar graphs, qualitative data to be in report format
Who will be responsible for creating the presentation of data?	Project team support analyst
Who is the audience for the results of the data?	Category team and procurement leadership team

Figure 2.9 Data collection questions

So what?

Many take the practice of data gathering for granted and assume it is an 'administrative' or 'junior' task associated with or allocated to an 'analyst'. However, the quality and depth of the data are critical inputs into the category management process, and therefore data gathering requires a forensic and experienced perspective. Care should be taken in ascertaining the most suitable 'owner' for each of the data-gathering activities identified.

Reliable and applicable data will help to build an effective category strategy plan and highlight opportunities to leverage value and business benefits. Therefore, data need to be collated in a timely manner, as well as be accurate, reliable and appropriate.

Category management application

- Forms the basis for category analysis and the category strategy plan
- Makes ownership of data-gathering tasks clearly visible to the category team
- Provides momentum for the category team through the action plan framework
- Is a how, what, when, where, why approach to category data collection

Limitations

The usefulness of the data collected is reliant upon the structure and the expertise of those assembling it. 'Garbage in, garbage out' is a common feature of a laissez-faire approach to this discipline. The data should also be continually assessed, as out-of-date material can be an issue and have a knock-on impact, but regrettably once the category management programme is in flow, this undertaking may be overlooked.

Although the information gleaned from the data-gathering process forms the bedrock of the category plan, as stated earlier, this task can be viewed as a routine or transactional activity by some. Unfortunately, as a result, data gathering can be afforded less priority and focus by expeditious category managers. This leads to less effort given to interpreting data and consequently less value being derived.

Template

The following template can be used to support category management data-gathering activities:

- Template 10: Data-gathering action plan

Activity 11
KEY SUPPLIER PROFILE

Section	Subsection	Information
Supplier contact information	Name of company	
	Address of company	
	Phone number	
	Web address	
	Key contacts/e-mail	
General supplier information	Company type/structure	
	Geographic coverage	
	Main sites	
	Number of employees	
Business strategy	Vision, goals and strategy	
Financial highlights	• Annual Sales revenues by key product ($m) • Sales • Net profit ($m/%) • Profit trend	
Products and services	Product and service offerings	
	Key markets/industry sectors served	
	Top five competitors	
Key customers	Top five customers	
	Customer references	
	Contracts with our organisation	
	• Total spend with our organisation • Our organisation spend trend	
	Relative importance to our organisation's business to supplier	
	Supplier preferencing analysis	
	Power/dependency profiling	
Additional info	Any other relevant info	
Summary	Implications for category strategy	

Figure 2.10   Key supplier profile

46

Overview

The purpose of the key supplier profile is to review each of the main suppliers operating within the supply markets that are aligned with the category. It is a deep analysis of both incumbent and prospective suppliers, and in particular an evaluation of the main players that might impact upon capacity or pricing conditions.

This profile is complementary to the category profile (Activity 9) and is an activity that is commonly undertaken in parallel. Each main supplier is researched in detail so that an understanding of its capabilities and market power can be assessed, which, in turn, should help the category manager to estimate how much leverage the category team may have when developing and implementing the category strategy.

Elements

The key supplier profile is based on a templated methodology that is designed to gather significant information on each main provider. The focus of the analysis concentrates on the following:

- **Business overview** – This section should provide an overview of the supplier and their product/service offerings. It is important to gain an understanding of whether the organisation is achieving growth in sales and profitability, and whether it is maintaining its position within the marketplace. As well as its product/service portfolio and financial structure, other facets that may be investigated include business strategy, marketing plans and environmental policy.
- **Market positioning** – This section outlines a high-level view of the supplier's standing within the marketplace. Analysis may include market share, key customers, growth, power, dominance and drivers. A more detailed look at the market is carried out separately in the next stage of the category management process.
- **Capacity** – This may relate to manufacturing and production, warehousing, distribution or other resources needed to deliver the goods/services. Over- or undercapacity will have a direct impact upon the ability to deliver the category strategy.
- **Financials** – This section constitutes a brief summary of key financial highlights, including an outline of the income statement and balance sheet, together with any key financial ratios and trends that are of significance.
- **Costs** – It is often difficult to obtain the supplier's internal costings related to the price of the product. However, depending upon the type and nature of the relationship, it may be that an 'open-book' procedure or variations thereof maybe in existence or could be developed, facilitating the sharing of this valuable information. This section acts as a precursor to PPCA (Activity 14).
- **Performance** – This area is frequently compared with business requirements (i.e. RAQSCI). Historical trend data including performance metrics, service levels and scorecards may be collated on incumbent suppliers in order to

reveal the supplier's historic level of commitment and quality of delivery against contract.

Risk profile – A general level of 'due diligence' should be undertaken with key outputs highlighted, together with any key risks. Some organisations like to provide a risk rating for each potential supplier in the category, while others will simply list the key risks associated with a supplier. Key risk areas might include finance, compliance, technology, supply chain, processes and resources.

Sustainability – There should be a summary of the supplier's strategy and contributions towards sustainability, including accreditations, carbon foot-print, emissions, waste-reduction initiatives and so on. These should be made relevant to the category and not general in nature.

Relationship – As this is often considered a 'soft' area and difficult to quan-tify, the state of the relationship can be a challenge, albeit valuable, to assess. Much of the information collected is likely to be of a qualitative nature and therefore subjective; however, it can provide a general picture of how the two parties have managed their business relationship to date.

Motivation – These data are generally gathered from the market grapevine (e.g. supplier contacts and trade magazines). It is an attempt to understand the supplier's motivation for retaining or gaining the buyer's business, such as spare capacity and brand attractiveness.

So what?

An in-depth study of the main suppliers within a category will support the team in establishing its initial ideas about market structure, levels of competition and the overall category strategy. This in turn will highlight relevant issues that could impinge upon the delivery of a category project. Ideally there should be sufficient number of suppliers to engender competition.

A comprehensive review of the suppliers combined with a thorough study of the supply market will provide a stable foundation for the category strategy to be built. It is complementary to the category profile, and the two together provide a platform from which the category strategy can be developed.

Category management application

- Supports the development of the category strategy
- Complements the category profile analysis
- Provides a foundation for an initial evaluation of the potential supply market
- Assists with opportunity/leverage identification

Limitations

As with other profile templates, there is a concern that the research element of the category management process can become a 'form-filling' exercise and be resource heavy in terms of the amount of analysis required to complete it. Some organisations believe that the category profile, key supplier profile and supply and value-chain analysis templates overlap each other, and so a 'lite' version is sometimes introduced where all three profile documents are combined.

However, critics of this approach argue that this can decrease 'attention to detail' and that important relevant factors may be missed as a result. Some category teams can become obsessed with filling in templates rather than focusing on the underlying research analysis required to unlock value in a marketplace.

Template

The following template can be used to gather detailed information on suppliers:

- Template 11: Key supplier profile

Activity 12
DAY ONE ANALYSIS

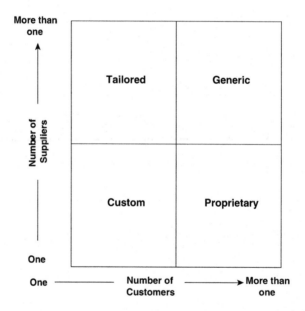

Figure 2.11   Day one analysis

Overview

Initially devised as a marketing tool to support brand campaigns in the 1980s, day one analysis was soon picked up by the procurement community and adapted to support the category management process. There are many iterations of this 2 x 2 matrix, the most popular being QPA Consultants' version from the 1990s.

The theoretical concept is that preliminary analysis related to product/market positioning can capture a 'day one snapshot' of the supply and demand variables that need to be considered. This in turn may prompt further thinking around potential programme issues that could arise during the category management process.

Elements

The day one analysis tool maps categories in relation to the 'number of suppliers' (in the supply market) on the y axis and 'number of customers' (of the product/service) on the x axis. It is designed in this way so that a 'rough plot' of a category can be made in order to assess quickly possible project difficulties, such as little negotiation leverage due to lack of suppliers but high customer demand.

Each quadrant represents a type of procurement together with its corresponding characteristics:

Tailored – This relates to products that are made uniquely for an organisation or a specific sector. There are likely to be many suppliers in the market capable of producing the offering; however, they will need to work collaboratively with the buyer to develop the specialist requirement. The emphasis of this type of buyer-supplier relationship revolves around joint understanding, supplier expertise and the development process.

Generic – This refers to a fairly commonly specified, standard 'off-the-shelf' product, for which there are many customers and suppliers. There is likely to be little market difficulty in obtaining the requirements and little need to cultivate a buyer-supplier relationship.

Custom – This relates to products made specifically by one supplier for one buyer. A high degree of trust, openness and honesty is needed to make this buyer-supplier relationship work effectively. The uniqueness of the product could bring capacity, capability and legal issues, such as intellectual property rights (IPR) retention, with it.

Proprietary – This refers to a supplier that has achieved and protected unique features in what they supply, but within a market that possesses many buyers. The buyer will need to become a 'buyer of choice' and develop a relationship whereby the supplier perceives that the arrangement will yield significant benefit over and above others that may be available.

So what?

As a method for mapping categories against supply and demand parameters, it helps category managers identify where maximum value may be gained at a very early stage in the category management process. For example, products that sit within the generic quadrant, where there are many buyers and sellers, are likely to be easier to source and negotiate compared to those that sit in the proprietary quadrant, where the supplier dominates the market with a specific product characteristic and therefore may dictate price to its many suppliers – a monopoly situation.

Undertaking a quick 'snapshot' enables hypothetical links to be established more quickly, which may reduce the overall category management process time devoted to preparation and planning.

Category management application

*   Establishes an initial 'snapshot' of potential supply issues
*   Can be used to develop early thinking around problems that could arise in the category management process
*   Is a mechanism for identifying categories in relation to supply and demand variables
*   Links to the Kraljic matrix (see Activity 19) and corresponding analysis

Limitations

Since its inception in the 1990s, day one analysis has become less popular over recent decades. Critics argue that it is superficial and insubstantial and therefore not worth the effort of completing, especially when the Kraljic matrix, a tool which is altogether better known and understood as part of the category management process, can be used instead at a later stage.

Some of the well-known players in the field of category management consultancy have dropped the technique from their defined methodologies, focusing more on frameworks that deliver distinct quantifiable output, although there are a few that maintain that day one analysis is integral to the preparation process.

As the majority of category management processes can include over 40 different models, tools and templates, accepted practice amongst practitioners tends to be 'sized to suit'. Therefore, relatively simple category projects are likely to drop the day one analysis, while more complex ones are more likely to preserve the matrix.

Template

The following template can be used to support category strategy development:

*   Template 12: Day one analysis

Activity 13
SITUATIONAL ANALYSIS (STP)

Figure 2.12 Situational analysis

Overview

Dr Fred Fosmire, an American academic with a thriving consulting practice, was the first to coin the problem-solving term STP in the 1960s. He is widely acknowledged as the progenitor of this technique. STP is a three-letter acronym which stands for situation, target, proposal. It is sometimes confused with the marketing STP process which stands for segmentation, targeting, positioning.

STP is a popular consulting technique used to gauge understanding of client issues, agree potential targets and develop a range of proposals. Fosmire argued that in order to effectively solve a problem, one must first understand the current situation in detail before putting forward a solution.

A number of variants on STP exist – for example, STPP, which includes a 'plan'; STPB, which includes 'benefits'; and STPR, which includes 'resources'.

Elements

According to Fosmire, problems and conflicts generally result from differences in three categories:

Facts – These are contributing and impeding forces. There are forces at work in the situation that help move towards the goal, and forces at work that impede movement towards the goal. Disagreements about the facts can be, for example, one person thinking one thing has happened, while another person has a different view of the situation.

Values/priorities – These are differences in priorities and values. One person thinks one thing is important, while someone else thinks something else should take precedence.

Solutions – We may agree on facts and priorities, but have different methods or plans to solve the problem.

The STP problem-solving technique was principally designed to flush out the facts of a situation before envisioning what the 'end state' might look like, and thus an accompanying solution can be developed. It is vital that the problem is clearly defined by all parties at the outset; otherwise this could skew the resulting questions and thus the data collected. The key components and related questions that might be used to facilitate STP are listed in Figure 2.13.

STP	Activity	Example questions
Situation	Describing the situation Gathering facts	• What are the facts? • What exactly is the situation? • What has been done? • Who is involved? • What are the people that are involved doing?
Target	Creating a vision Defining the vision	• What does success look like? • How will we know when we have achieved it? • Is this a stretch target?
Proposal	Exploring possibilities Analysing options Clarifying priorities	• What are the pros and cons of each possibility? • What is the cost of each? • What are the consequences of not acting? • Who is committed to carrying out the solution? • Which option will bring 'quick wins'?

Figure 2.13 STP explained

So what?

The STP process is a succinct way of engaging business stakeholders. It is often used as a means of creating support cross-functionally through the deployment of a facilitated 'brainstorming' session.

Once the problem has been clearly defined, the category manager can act as an objective mediator, helping develop and channel the STP questioning process. The questions and responses need to be continually reviewed and refined throughout, and strong facilitation skills are needed to ensure the robustness of this activity.

The output of this technique can provide invaluable information that can inform the category plan. It will also help the procurement team understand the appetite for the resulting project from within the business and any potential issues they may face from a political perspective.

Category management application

- Provides a way of problem solving with stakeholders
- Provides a universal understanding of goals and objectives
- Engages and enlists key stakeholder support
- Allows procurement to be viewed as objective
- Can capture 'roadblocks' to the project early
- Will inform the early stages of the category-planning process by way of its output

Limitations

It is difficult to find many who would criticise STP, as it is a useful problem-solving tool. However, a recent prognosis amongst senior procurement practitioners is that while it is sufficient at gathering data at a surface level, the analysis does not go to the depth required in today's more complex, multifaceted organisations. It is increasingly becoming regarded as only a 'first step' in terms of mining the data required to initiate the category plan. Its application would appear to be more popular as a rapport- or relationship-building tool than that of a serious piece of research aimed at feeding the category strategy.

The STP process will need to be managed carefully, as procurement does not want to be seen to be 'steering the solution'. The success of the outcome is heavily dependent upon the facilitation skills of the category manager. If these skills are not in situ, then the final document can be vague and open to interpretation, and therefore its creditability will be diminished.

Template

The following template can be used as a problem-solving technique:

- Template 13: STP

Activity 14
PURCHASE-PRICE COST ANALYSIS (PPCA)

Type of product/service	Supplier evaluated		Date completed		
Cost build-up	Currency	Fixed costs	Semi-fixed/Semi-variable costs	Variable costs	Total costs
Labour costs					
	Total labour costs				
Material costs					
	Total material costs				
Production costs					
	Total production costs				
Logistics costs					
	Total logistics costs				
Overhead costs					
	Total overhead costs				
	Gross profits				
	Net profits				
	Totals				
			Current selling price		

Figure 2.14 Purchase-price cost analysis

Overview

PPCA is a popular tool initially developed by the accounting community in the 1970s and subsequently tailored by purchasing consultants in the 1980s. It is primarily used to identify the breakdown of costs involved in the production of a product. This in turn helps with further research in relation to pricing (e.g. the amount of profit retained by the supplier).

This technique is also referred to as cost-breakdown analysis or 'teardown' analysis, and it is considered that understanding such detail can be helpful when it comes to the implementation and negotiation stages of the category management process, as it helps the buying team to challenge quoted prices. It also helps form the foundation of open-book collaboration and supplier development processes. However, PPCA is not appropriate for all procurement scenarios (e.g. a monopoly market structure).

Elements

Obtaining precise information from suppliers can prove difficult; therefore, when operating the tool, assumptions are often made. There is an effort-reward equation about obtaining some cost information, which inevitably means that at best the output will only be an estimation of the breakdown of costs and profit. Where longer-term collaborative relationships exist in the supply base, it pays to take an iterative approach to PPCA and therefore hone in on a more accurate cost breakdown through subsequent revisions as new cost data are established.

The key elements of a PPCA are as follows:

Material costs – These may include the raw materials to make a product and any other materials, such as semifinished goods, components or subassemblies used in the production process, plus packaging and waste.

Labour costs – These may include contracted and subcontracted labour (full or part time) directly associated with the production of the finished goods.

Production costs – These may include the operating costs of equipment, plus any associated repairs, maintenance, energy or utilities, but should not include depreciation on capital equipment or any duplication with overheads.

Logistics costs – These may include materials handling, haulage, warehousing, freight and associated export costs.

Overheads – These will include all indirect costs appropriately attributed to the finished product, possibly including shared service costs (HR and procurement), financing costs, sales and marketing, general management and so forth.

Profits – This is the net operating profit.

Selling Price – This is the price at which the product is to be sold.

Much of the information needed to complete the PPCA can be sourced from industry journals, supply contracts, annual accounts, sales contacts, external benchmarking clubs and so on. Once all of the costs have been pinpointed and classified, a profit calculation can be made by reviewing the differential between costs and selling price. Finished goods can be broken down using reverse-engineering techniques to establish the component parts and a cost breakdown estimate established.

So what?

Breaking down product costs will help the category team plan their category strategy. Even if the information is just a 'rough guide' estimate, it is still relevant and may offer some form of confidence when analysing and determining the supplier's pricing expectations.

Obtaining the information in the first instance can be daunting, and it is recommended that category teams view the analysis as 'basic but developable', depending upon the amount of time and effort available. This undertaking is usually done in teams, so that a breadth of experience is drawn from and utilised in order to populate the PPCA template.

For longer-term purchases (especially in manufacturing and lean production environments), PPCA can be an incredibly powerful tool to establish the 'should cost' of a product. This gives the buyer significant insight and advantage during the category planning and supplier negotiation phases. It is also an essential leverage tool to support supplier development and continuous improvement programmes.

Category management application

- Supports the preparation and research stage of category management
- Provides insight into the supplier's cost structure
- Can assist with any negotiation elements of the category management process
- Affords a basis for benchmarking and continuous improvement
- May provide the basis for open-book costing and collaboration in the long term

Limitations

Some authors of category management texts believe that buyers seem to 'shy away' from developing a PPCA, due to the potential complexity and enormity of the task. There also appears to be a commonly held misconception that to create a credible cost breakdown, the document owner needs to have financial expertise and access to accurate supplier data, opposed to attempting an estimated version, as described earlier. Many consultants will use these arguments to justify their involvement in the process.

Initially, PPCA as part of the category management process was only ever meant to be at a rudimentary level and not a detailed accounting exercise. However, this is also exactly the reason why some category teams decide not to deploy the practice, as the output is seen as merely a poor approximation and therefore a waste of valuable resources.

PPCA is highly applicable to products and finished goods, but it is a lot harder to apply to services. The principles are fully transferable but the associated cost breakdown for services is more difficult to establish accurately.

Finally, it is worth remembering that if the PPCA output is to be used to contest a supplier's price, then as much factual evidence should be gathered as possible, as a failure to do this could mean that your credibility is undermined when negotiating or collaborating with suppliers in that category.

Template

The following template can be used to support the identification of supplier costs and profits:

•   Template 14: Purchase-price cost analysis

STAGE 3

Analysis

Overview and benefits of this stage

At the heart of category management is the pursuit of an overarching strategy to manage corporate expenditure. The strategy needs to be both dynamic and flexible in order to adapt to changes in the competitive environment, hence the need for an iterative approach. Often the base facts and data within a category do not change much over the short term, but external markets can change rapidly, and so the overarching strategy for the category needs to change accordingly.

This stage of category management can be one of the most rewarding and challenging sets of activities within the full end-to-end process. To be certain of adding value, an accurate fact base and solid foundation of research are essential. This will lead to the creation of a category strategy that delivers breakthrough value. Taking a shortcut at this stage will only lead to short-sighted strategies based on limited understanding.

The ultimate goal of this stage of the category management process is therefore to understand in detail how the external market operates and, consequently, how cost and value are generated. The stage comprises a series of analytical tools and techniques designed to give insight into how the external market works so that a strategy is able to be created.

Some category management processes combine this stage with either the one preceding it (Research) or the one immediately afterwards (Strategy). How the process is partitioned up is very much secondary to the importance of ensuring that analysis is undertaken. We believe analysis constitutes a separate stage of category management in its own right because of the need for gateway approval during the process. This is particularly the case for larger, higher-value and more complex categories where senior management support and approval should be given to ensure that sufficient analysis has been undertaken to support the following strategy-creation activities.

Some organisations outsource their analysis activities to third-party consultants. While this is appealing – and often consultants are more capable of creating an insightful analysis than existing in-house resources – there are risks attached to this. In effect, you are placing the seeds of your category strategy into the hands of a third party. It may be expeditious from a resourcing point of view, but there is the potential to lose knowledge and understanding about the category. It does little to engage and educate stakeholders in the dynamics of the market.

Extra explanation and theory

In this section of the handbook we offer six of the most commonly used analytical tools in category management. You would typically find each of these in any professional category management process; in fact, some practitioners believe these models constitute the heart of category management.

As we have already mentioned, the purpose of this stage is to analyse both the internal and external environments of the category and to 'converge' this analysis into a single view of the current situation and circumstances. Many theorists refer to this as the 'strategic position'. In effect we are taking three perspectives of the category (the internal analysis, the analysis of our competitors and the analysis of our supply markets) to form a triage of assessment (see Figure 3.1).

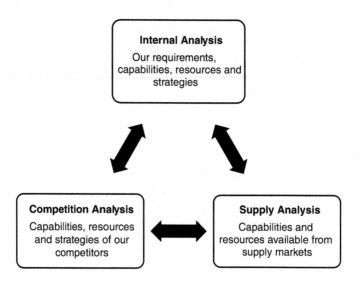

Figure 3.1 Category analysis triage

As with all tools and theoretical constructs, there are advantages and disadvantages with each academic model. Professor Andrew Cox is one of the fiercest advocates of contingent circumstances playing a governing role regarding the appropriateness of any business tool or technique. His argument is essentially one of *context*, which is why the preceding stage, Research, is so fundamentally important.

The six models that we present in this stage can each provide a somewhat simplistic perspective on the category (although there is nothing simple about supply and value-chain analysis, nor competition analysis for that matter, provided they are conducted with rigour). However, when taken together, the combined effect is far more illuminating.

The best example of this is the comparison of the analyses that come from Kraljic portfolio analysis (Activity 19) and supplier preferencing (Activity 20). On their own they present a somewhat biased view (either the buyer's or the supplier's perspective). However, when taken together and cross-referenced, the full dynamic of the analysis of the category can be seen, as illustrated in Figure 3.2.

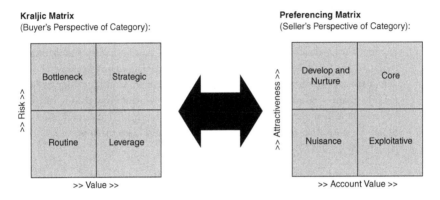

Figure 3.2 Comparative portfolio analysis

This comparative analysis is explored further in Stage 4 (Strategy) – for example in Activities 21 and 22 – when specific strategies start to be identified and assessed.

Thus, there is a smooth transition of category strategy development that started in Stage 2 (Research), passing steadily through Stage 3 (Analysis) until the full set of strategic options are identified and evaluated in Stage 4 (Strategy).

As with each of these stages, it is essential that the same category management team stays with the journey of development and that detailed data records are developed and stored. While the first iteration of research, analysis and strategy may be fairly time-consuming, there is a distinct advantage in reviewing the previous work of category teams when going through the second, third or fourth iteration of category management.

Practical hints and tips

1   Analysis tools may be used to generate a 'view' of the market, including its evolution, current position and likely future changes. Use primary and secondary sources of data to collate your market intelligence. Analyse, filter and verify the information as part of the process.

2   Use the tools and templates provided in this handbook. This will give you consistency with other category management initiatives and also provide a 'best-practice' foundation to your project.

3   Seek the assistance of relevant stakeholders to interpret and incorporate the intelligence into the category strategy. Identify whether the market profile is neutral, positive or negative for you.

4   Regularly review and update your analysis tools to ensure the intelligence remains current.

5   A failure to maintain up-to-date and ongoing intelligence on dynamic supply markets will prevent you from making informed category decisions.

6   A lack of environmental scanning prevents the ability to adapt category strategies in response to changing supply-market conditions.

7   Be sure to include stakeholders who will perform the tasks of collating and analysing relevant market data, particularly technical or other subject-matter experts. This will allow them to be involved in your category management initiative and to leverage their experience and specialist knowledge.

8   There are many techniques for finding out information. Consider using 'request for information' enquiries or even a collaborative workshop with one or more key suppliers. Tear-down analysis or reverse-engineering activities may also help.

9   Store the outputs in your shared project folder and keep them secure.

Summary of activities

There are six key activities outlined within this stage of the category management process:

1   **SWOT** – This is a simple analytical tool to establish the internal strengths and weaknesses of the organisational expenditure, together with the external opportunities and threats within the category.

2   **Macroenvironmental analysis (STEEPLE)** – This is a macroenvironmental scanning framework to analyse the external influences on the category markets.

3   **Competition analysis** – This is a review of the competitive forces that exist both within the market and throughout the supply chain, which give an insight into the profit potential that may exist within any given category market.

4   **Supply and value-chain analysis** – This is the process of identifying, mapping and analysing the costs and value that reside within the category's primary supply chain so that (later) value-extracting strategies can be developed.

5   **Kraljic portfolio analysis** – This is a variation on the original portfolio approach towards supply management developed by Dr Peter Kraljic. This fundamental analysis reviews the category from the buyer's perspective.

6   **Supplier preferencing** – This is the counteracting analysis to Kraljic's review, which takes on board an estimation of the suppliers' perspectives of the buyer within any category.

What the gateway needs to consider

Similar to the preceding stage (Research), the temptation for category managers to take a shortcut and bypass a methodical and structured approach to market analysis is extremely high. If this happens, there is a risk that any subsequent category strategy is based on unfounded assumptions, which could in turn jeopardise the value of the outputs from the category management initiative. In effect, managers are simply making snap judgements about the category based on their limited understanding of how it works.

This can be difficult to argue with an experienced team, particularly if the people involved have worked in a market for more than five years or so. However, the discipline of working through the analysis with all stakeholders is essential. This needs to be an inclusive exercise, where even the dumbest questions (what if, how about, how does that work? etc.) are encouraged and actively explored.

We recommend that a specific approval point (gateway) is considered at the end of Stage 3 (Analysis), where the emphasis must be on whether the category analysis undertaken is sufficiently robust to commence the development of a category strategy. The inclusion of a 'go/no-go' decision helps to control the category team and ensure that sufficient focus is given to robust analysis without jumping ahead to premature conclusions.

The following checklist gives some more practical guidance on what the category manager should be preparing for the Stage 3 gateway.

Gateway approval checklist

STAGE 3: ANALYSIS

1. Has the supply market been reviewed using appropriate market analysis tools?

2. Have the relative structures of power and dependency within the supply market been analysed?

3. Have the external macro- and microenvironments been analysed using appropriate environmental analysis tools?

4. Have all social responsibility, ethical and environmental factors been analysed for the category?

5. Have all relevant stakeholders given input into the category analysis?

6. Is there an appetite and mandate for change internally?

7. Have the risk register and project plan been reviewed and updated?

8. Has the situational analysis (STP) been updated?

Signed: _____

Category Manager

_____

Sponsor

Activity 15
SWOT

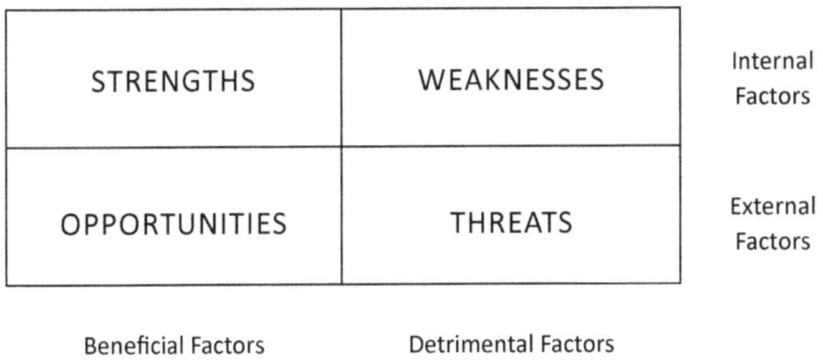

STRENGTHS	WEAKNESSES	Internal Factors
OPPORTUNITIES	THREATS	External Factors

Beneficial Factors　　　Detrimental Factors

Figure 3.3 SWOT analysis

Overview

SWOT analysis emanated from the Stanford Research Institute in the mid-1960s. The model is a mnemonic (for strengths, weaknesses, opportunities and threats) representing the factors to consider when assessing a business or a proposition. It is a popular analysis tool within the category management process, as it helps the category team explore existing and new suppliers, as well as gain a perspective on the team's possible leverage/negotiation position.

Elements

SWOT analysis necessitates an understanding both of an organisation's environment and of its resource capabilities. The matrix is divided into four key areas:

Strengths – These are positive internal attributes (e.g. highly skilled staff, intellectual property rights and corporate brand).

Weaknesses – These are the internal weaknesses of the organisation (e.g. high overheads, old technology and poor internal processes).

Opportunities – These are external factors that could influence the organisation (e.g. a supplier with an opportunity to introduce cost savings into the category).

Threats – These are external risk factors (e.g. the threat of consolidation in the supply market, thus reducing the number of suppliers available to work with).

So what?

SWOT analysis is normally used in conjunction with a range of other analytical tools as part of the overall category management process.

It is often used to evaluate organisations; however, it can also be used on oneself for personal development purposes.

Category management application

- Highlights an organisation's strengths, which may help the category team develop a category plan
- Can determine what opportunities may be available for further exploration by the category team
- Reveals potential threats in the supply market which could adversely affect the category project
- Enables comparison of important factors between the buyer and its supplier organisations

Limitations

SWOT is purely a 'snapshot' in time of the status quo. It does not provide direction or next steps. Some critics have argued that SWOT is not really an analytical tool and that it is purely a framework to structure facts and data concerning the current situation.

It should be noted that there is overlap between SWOT and STEEPLE (Activity 16), albeit SWOT considers both internal and external factors, while STEEPLE only considers external influences.

Template

The following template can be used to support category analysis:

- Template 15: SWOT

Activity 16
MACROENVIRONMENTAL ANALYSIS (STEEPLE)

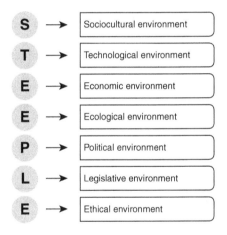

Figure 3.4 Macroenvironmental analysis

Overview

'STEEPLE' is a mnemonic representing the macroenvironmental factors that need to be considered when analysing a category. It is a framework for review particularly in relation to strategic planning, market positioning or category development.

Each of the letters within the 'STEEPLE' framework represents a different factor within the external environment (i.e. sociocultural, technological, economic, ecological, political, legislative and ethical) that, although beyond the organisation's direct control, is still an influence upon its activities.

The framework tends to be overused within business schools and has taken on many different forms over the years, including PEST (political, economic, sociocultural and technological), SLEPT (sociocultural, legislative, economic, political and technological) and PESTLE (political, economic, sociocultural, technological, legislative and ecological), amongst others. These differences are relatively minor, as each variant seems to incorporate the others' elements in some shape or form.

Elements

Each of the STEEPLE factors varies in significance depending upon the category being analysed; however, in general terms the elements are as follows:

Sociocultural environment – This highlights the importance of demographics, society and culture on a business.

Technological environment – This focuses on the rate of innovation and diffusion, as well as the development of technical standards.

Economic environment – This considers fiscal policies such as taxes, lending and exchange rates and inflation.

Ecological environment – This covers the influence of the natural world and the awareness of the demand for raw materials and the use of energy, as well as disposal of waste.

Political environment – This includes issues such as local and national government actions, trade relations and political stability.

Legislative environment – This covers legislation and regulations, including aspects of governance, contracts, compliance and public accountability.

Ethical environment – This includes ethical considerations, such as fair trade, ethical trade, modern slavery and bribery.

So what?

The STEEPLE template promotes proactive thinking rather than reliance upon habitual or instinctive reactions. By defining each environmental factor, this allows for a detailed review of potential impacts upon a category of spend.

STEEPLE analysis can help identify SWOT factors (Activity 15) and support the analysis required to understand an organisation's strategic position when developing category strategies.

Category management application

- Supports category analysis preparation prior to strategy development
- Aids understanding of macroenvironmental factors of existing and potential category supplier organisations
- Builds general commercial awareness
- Promotes wider thinking around potential risks associated with the category strategy

Limitations

It is important to identify and define the subject of STEEPLE analysis clearly; otherwise the resulting output could be too wide and varied to explore.

Many academics prefer the original PEST model, as it is thought that it offers more opportunity for strategic appreciation and analysis, rather than simply a longer list of headings.

Either way, it should be noted that this model is merely a list of headings, as opposed to an analytical or predictive tool in itself. It provides a useful guide and aides memory, but should not be relied on for much more than this.

Template

The following template can be used to support category analysis:

• Template 16: STEEPLE

Activity 17
COMPETITION ANALYSIS

Porter's five forces

Figure 3.5   Competition analysis

Source: adapted from Porter (1980)

Overview

Michael Porter (1980) originally developed the five-forces model as a way of evaluating the attractiveness (profit potential) of an industry. He described his analysis as being concerned with the 'forces driving industry competition'.

This model can aid the category strategy-development process. Assessing all facets of potential supply competition provides a rounded view when deciding upon what action to take in order to gain a competitive advantage.

Elements

In any industry, whether it is domestic or international, or whether it produces a product or a service, the rules of competition are embodied in five competitive forces that Porter classified as follows:

Threat of new entrants – This relates to the competitive pressures placed by new entrants to a market and the degree to which this can be prevented by *barriers to entry* (which are factors that new entrants to the market will need to overcome to be successful).

Bargaining power of suppliers – Where demand exceeds supply, the supply base will have greater bargaining power over buyers, particularly if there are no alternative sources of supply. It is essential to reduce as much dependency and competitive pressure from suppliers as possible.

Bargaining power of customers – Where supply exceeds demand from customers, or the demand is heavily consolidated, additional pressures will be placed upon the market. This will increase competition and reduce prices unless the customers' bargaining power can be negated.

Threat of substitutes – Alternative products and services increase competitive pressures on a market simply because they reduce the customers' dependency and give them more opportunity to switch to alternatives.

Rivalry within the market – Competition within the market will depend on just how saturated or dynamic the market is.

So what?

Lack of competition improves profit potential in a market. Category managers therefore need to understand how to develop supply-market opportunities for their categories in order to improve their overall leverage.

Correct application of this model should be at the lowest level of category hierarchy (i.e. at the granular, microindustry level); otherwise the output could be too 'broad brush' and thus potentially meaningless.

Category management application

- Provides an overview of supply and demand factors in operation and the impact on a category strategy
- Supports the development of supply-market analysis
- Highlights potential areas for market leverage
- Could stimulate market/supplier development strategies

Limitations

This model has been the subject of some critical comment, largely surrounding the static nature of the framework. Category management in comparison is a proactive, dynamic and ongoing process.

It has also been argued that category managers tend to 'fit' a strategy around Porter's five forces in order to accommodate the output, whereas a more modern approach is to 'stretch' a strategy – that is, be more lateral and forward thinking – in order to circumnavigate the market supply and demand parameters.

Template

The following template can be used to analyse market forces and rivalry that might impact a category strategy:

- Template 17: Porter's five forces

Activity 18

SUPPLY AND
VALUE-CHAIN ANALYSIS

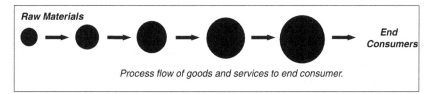

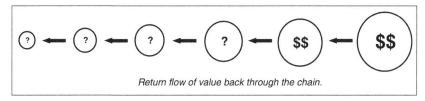

Figure 3.6   Supply and value-chain analysis

Overview

Supply and value-chain analysis is about the systematic breakdown and analysis of the primary supply chain at each tier so that opportunities to create value and mitigate risk can be identified. Arguably the theory supporting this can be traced back to Professor Michael Porter when he considered the competitive forces in a given market and then strung together the analyses of several markets in a supply chain to form the 'value network'.

Supply and value-chain analysis builds on Porter's concepts and incorporates supply-chain mapping, supply-chain analysis and value-chain analysis. It is essential that a clear distinction is made between primary and secondary (support) supply chains, with the focus remaining firmly on the primary (direct) supply chain.

Elements

There are five distinct stages required to develop a powerful and informative supply and value-chain analysis. These should be conducted sequentially, as follows:

1 **Supply-chain mapping** – This is a systematic breakdown of the primary supply chain to identify each stage (tier), both upstream and downstream of the organisation. This should be conducted at the organisational level, rather than at the activity level, and must include all stages (including agencies and distribution channels) regardless of what part each plays in the chain. The aim is full transparency of every organisation in the primary supply chain.
2 **Cost analysis** – This is a detailed, step-by-step breakdown of the costs of goods sold (COGS), working from the end consumer back to the origin of raw materials. Distinction needs to be made at each stage between selling price, profit, production costs, expenses and input costs for this analysis to be effective.
3 **Value analysis** – This is a detailed analysis of the breakdown and allocation of profit throughout the supply chain, together with a contrast (by ratio or equivalent) to the costs. An analysis of the causes for the profit should accompany each stage.
4 **Risk and resilience analysis** – This is a detailed analysis of the dependencies and vulnerabilities at each stage of the supply chain. This should be based on the likely impact on your own organisation in order for you to draw up a meaningful risk profile and to identify the overall supply-chain resilience.
5 **Opportunity analysis** – This is, finally, a review of the costs, value and risks at each stage to identify opportunities for enhancing value and reducing risk.

So what?

Supply and value-chain analysis is incredibly powerful when done well. It gives you a detailed breakdown and analysis of the costs, value added and risks associated with a specific category at each stage in the supply chain. This provides a valuable basis for identifying potential opportunities to create value and mitigate risk exposure.

Typical outputs could include opportunities to consolidate markets, integrate production stages, streamline processes, outsource/insource, disintermediate, renegotiate and so on.

Category management application

- Maps every stage in the production and supply of a category, giving full transparency and providence for buyers
- Provides valuable detailed financial data to support future operational reviews and customer-supplier negotiations
- Profiles the risk and resilience within the primary supply chain
- Identifies potential areas for delivering breakthrough value

Limitations

The greatest challenge with supply and value-chain analysis is the time and resource requirement that accompanies this activity; it can be lengthy and time-consuming. The biggest issue here is that if organisations try to short-circuit these issues, then the analysis will be suboptimised. Of course, consultants love this kind of activity because it can help justify charging a large fee to their clients.

It is essential that the focus remains on the primary supply chain and does not get diverted into secondary (support) supply chains (i.e. indirect expenditure). However, this is easier said than done, as in practice these can be hard to separate.

The person or organisation undertaking supply and value-chain analysis needs a high level of competence and knowledge. It requires perseverance to break down the supply-chain tiers and then a forensic approach to the cost and value analysis. While many organisations claim to have transparency throughout their supply chains, the reality is often very different – as has been witnessed with a number of high-profile supply-chain disasters. Obviously, should blockchain technology become more widely adopted, actual transparency would be more easily achieved.

Another limitation comes from the degree of interpretation that accompanies the value analysis. The financial cost analysis is tangible and objective, but the accompanying value analysis becomes a matter of subjective interpretation as to why one supply-chain partner is more (or less) profitable than others. You could be tempted to turn to the academic work of Professor Andrew Cox et al. (2002) for supporting theory on core competence and critical asset analysis in supply chains, but this work is challenging in itself.

Template

The following template can be used to support supply and value-chain analysis:

- Template 18: Supply and value-chain analysis

Activity 19
KRALJIC PORTFOLIO ANALYSIS

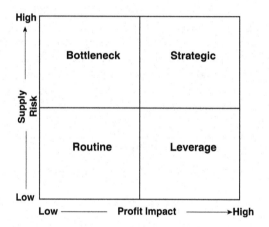

Figure 3.7 Kraljic portfolio analysis

Source: adapted from Kraljic (1983)

Overview

Dr Peter Kraljic was the first academic to bring portfolio models into the procurement arena. He developed his matrix in the early 1980s, with the aim of demonstrating how much time buyers should focus on managing different categories of expenditure within an organisation.

The matrix is based on two dimensions: a simplified classification of an organisation's expenditure on goods and services in terms of the profit potential, and supply risk.

Elements

The two key dimensions can be defined as follows:

- **Profit impact** – This is the strategic importance of procurement in terms of the value added by product line, the percentage of raw materials in total costs and their impact on profitability.
- **Supply risk** – This is the complexity of the supply market gauged by supply scarcity, pace of technology and materials substitution, entry barriers, logistics cost or complexity and monopoly or oligopoly conditions.

These dimensions are used to determine how categories of expenditure might be managed:

Bottleneck – Products that can only be acquired from a limited source of supply or where there is a high degree of supply risk. Suppliers need to be managed in order to secure delivery. This quadrant is typically characterised by bespoke/rolling contracts.

Strategic – Products that are crucial to the firm and are characterised by high value and high supply risk. Suppliers need to be closely managed. This quadrant is typically characterised by strategic-partnering relationships.

Routine – Products that are easy to acquire and have a relatively low impact in the event of nondelivery. The buyers' efforts should concentrate on implementing standardised ordering procedures and improving efficiency. This quadrant is typically characterised by volume/blanket agreements.

Leverage – Products that are easy to buy and could result in significant cost savings due to high volume/values, thus greatly impacting contribution to the bottom line. This quadrant is characterised by many suppliers and quality is standardised, therefore encouraging frequent tendering.

So what?

Kraljic's matrix is used extensively within the procurement and supply-chain arena. It is often carried out at the planning stages when developing a sourcing strategy for either the function or individual categories of expenditure.

Some debate has been generated about whether the model assesses categories of expenditure or individual supplier relationships. Although Kraljic intended the former, there is some application to the latter in specific circumstances.

Many consulting firms have adapted or oversimplified Kraljic's matrix in an attempt to pass off the model as their own. Although it has sometimes been referred to as 'supply positioning' and been attributed different titles for its quadrants, the principles laid down by Kraljic remain the same.

Category management application

- Assists in the development of category management strategies
- Aids both supplier and supply-market analysis
- Supports spend analysis
- Provides focus to category management activities

Limitations

Kraljic's matrix has generated much discussion and debate, with some claiming it to be a panacea and others considering it to be extremely limited in application.

The model is only a 'snapshot' in time, and from a practical perspective it does not consider the resources needed to appropriately manage the suppliers of the products in each of the quadrants.

Some academics have argued that the axis definitions need to be precise in order to collate meaningful data and that too much subjectivity can occur when application occurs. Linked to this, one sustained criticism is that this model is only based on the buyer's perspective of the purchases.

Some consulting firms believe the axes should be graded, consequently allowing items to be plotted on the matrix like a statistical graph – but this is probably an extension too far beyond Kraljic's original intention and there are risks inherent in this approach.

Template

The following template can be used to segment categories of expenditure:

- Template 19: Kraljic matrix

Activity 20
SUPPLIER PREFERENCING

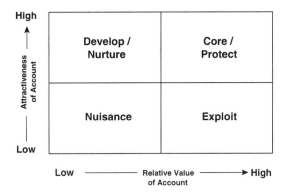

Figure 3.8 Supplier preferencing

Source: adapted from Steele and Court (1996)

Overview

Originated by Paul Steele and Brian Court in the mid-1990s, this model enables procurement functions to understand how a supplier might value its account with them. It suggests that from the supplier's perspective there is a correlation between the attractiveness of the buyer's account and the revenue generated, which in turn affects how the supplier will manage its account with the buyer.

In many ways, this matrix provides a counterview to the Kraljic matrix in that it is a representation of the supplier's perspective of business.

Elements

The horizontal axis of the matrix is represented by the relative value of business to the supplier, which serves as a measure of potential revenue. The vertical axis of the matrix represents the attractiveness of the account, which can be quantified in terms of prestige, future business and so on. Each quadrant can be interpreted as follows:

Develop/nurture – These are accounts that bring little in terms of value to a supplier but are very attractive in terms of potential. They are often seen as the supplier's future, and much focus is placed on developing this segment of customer relationships.

Core/protect – These are accounts of both high value and high attractiveness. They are seen as core business, and the supplier places emphasis on levels of service in order to defend its position, while attempting to increase business.

Nuisance – These are organisations that bring little in terms of value and potential. In this case the supplier might be expected to show little interest or support, and may be actively making efforts to withdraw.

Exploit – These are organisations that may have a high volume of sales, forming substantial revenue, albeit from an account that is not considered to be attractive. In this case, the supplier may concentrate on driving short-term benefits, as retaining the long-term relationship is not considered important.

So what?

This is a useful segmentation model for category managers. It provides a counterperspective to Kraljic's purchasing portfolio matrix and can help explain a supplier's approach towards customer relationship management.

The procurement function can use the outputs from the segmentation exercise to orientate resources and inform decisions in relation to category and supplier relationship-management strategies, amongst others.

Category management application

- Assists in the development of category management strategies
- Aids both supplier and supply-market analysis
- Provides focus to category management activities
- Helps interpret supplier behaviour

Limitations

One of the obvious limitations of this particular model is that it is predicated totally on guesswork. The category manager is required to make assumptions as to how attractive the account might or might not be, as well as what the value of the account is in relation to the supplier's other accounts. From here, the category manager then is expected to use this model to second-guess how the supplier will react.

Some criticism has also been levied at the terms given to the two lower quadrants. The model was developed in the mid-1990s, and since this time, greater emphasis has been placed on customer service and account management. While the model may contain some truisms, the notion that suppliers will treat some customers as a nuisance, while exploiting others, is disingenuous to most modern service-based organisations.

Finally, although billed as a counterview of Kraljic's matrix, care should be taken when comparing the outputs of these two models. Kraljic's focus is about profiling a category of expenditure, while supplier preferencing is about profiling a specific supplier's account-management style. The two are very different and should not be automatically cross-referenced.

Template

The following template can be used to understand the suppliers' perspective:

- Template 20: Supplier preferencing

STAGE 4

Strategy

Overview and benefits of this stage

This stage represents the heart of the category management process and some would argue its very purpose. Each of the three stages preceding this stage have been building up to this point in time. A 'good' strategy is predicated on diligent research and critical analysis, and without the necessary prior investment in these areas, you cannot expect to develop an effective category strategy.

The kind of strategy we are talking about here refers to a long-term plan to manage the spend within any given category; it is obviously not referring to a short-term plan to source a new supplier! This may sound somewhat patronising, but it is a distinction that strikes at the heart of many of the current operational issues within category management (i.e. the confusion that some procurement people seem to have between 'strategy' and 'sourcing'). We need to reemphasise that sourcing and category management are different processes with different outcomes; the two are far from synonymous.

Sourcing refers to the gathering of requirements, researching a supply market and obtaining competitive bids from a range of capable suppliers so that contracts can be placed with the best overall providers. It is relatively short term and involves competitive bidding from the supply market. Category management may sound similar, but it is far broader than this. One of the outputs of a category strategy could be the sourcing of a new contract with a supplier – but this would be just one initiative amongst a range of others, which over time map out a strategic plan to manage the category spend.

A category strategy could therefore result in a wide range of solutions – not just sourcing. Some of these potential solutions might include:

*   renegotiation of existing/new deals;
*   outsourcing/insourcing;

- offshoring/reshoring;
- joint ventures with others;
- supplier relationship management;
- new product development;
- process improvement;
- demand management;
- product substitution;
- business process reengineering;
- vertical integration;
- supply-chain disintermediation;
- supply-base rationalisation;
- automation, and so on.

There are many options and solutions available, and these are explored further when we discuss the category strategy cube next. For now, we simply want to make it clear that the outcome of a category strategy is not just sourcing; it should be far broader than this narrow procurement-oriented focus. It should also be obvious that category management processes that automatically build in sourcing activities (e.g. the current CIPS category management process and others) are flawed and short-sighted. Members of the category management team must not limit themselves in their thinking during the strategy stage. The category strategy should consider all possible solutions and then pull together a long-term plan for the overall spend within the category.

This long-term plan might contain a series of initiatives over time to manage the category spend. A simplified example is shown in Figure 4.1.

Initiative	Time frame	Target
1. Harmonise prices across all existing suppliers.	Month 1	$10k cost savings
2. Run eRFx to rationalise supply base to three preferred suppliers.	Month 2	$45k cost savings
3. Demand management exercise with stakeholders.	Months 3–6	$10k spend reduction
4. Search for low-cost country (LCC) alternative.	Months 6–9	N/A
5. Renegotiate with preferred suppliers.	Month 9	$25k price reduction 10% service improvements
6. Switch 30% supply to LCC alternative and reduce to two domestic preferred suppliers.	Months 12–18	$40k price reduction

Figure 4.1 Example category strategy plan

Initiative	Time frame	Target
7. Introduce supplier relationship management (SRM) programme.	Month 18+	N/A
8. Make continuous process improvements.	Months 24–48	$30k cost reduction 20% quality improvements

Figure 4.1 Continued

Extra explanation and theory

The simplified example of a series of category-based initiatives helps demonstrate the nature of category strategy – that is that it is wider than sourcing alone, it is long term (typically three to five years), it contains several progressive initiatives and it delivers a number of business requirements (not just cost reduction). On top of this, it really should be flexible and have the ability to adapt to organisational and environmental changes around it.

This leads us to consider what we mean by a category *strategy*. 'Strategy' is an overused term in business and the source of much academic debate, some of which is unnecessary and valueless for the business world. In category management we are simply referring to a cross-functional, long-term plan to manage the category spend and achieve targeted business requirements. No doubt there will be some academic critics of this simple definition, but it is pragmatic and effective for category management.

Category management adopts a 'logical incrementalism' approach towards developing strategy (i.e. a planned approach to strategy making in a series of incremental steps), which gets reviewed and refined in subsequent iterations.

One of the popular modern-day approaches to strategy development is the PCA model (Johnson et al. 2014) outlined in Figure 4.2, now referred to as the 'exploring strategy model'. This is a dynamic and evolving model that considers three interdependent sets of activity in order to create and execute a strategy. The strategic positioning (P) activities can be likened to the research and analysis stages of category management, while the strategic choices (C) and strategic action (A) activities are similar to the strategy and implementation stages of category management.

Figure 4.2 PCA strategy-development model

Source: adapted from Johnson et al. (2014)

So, what are the dimensions of an effective category strategy? Here are some of the key features that category managers should be aiming for. A 'good' category strategy:

- is customer focused;
- has a long-term orientation (three to five years);
- is fully cross-functional/pan-enterprise;
- delivers 'breakthrough' business value;
- focuses on multiple deliverables (not just cost savings);
- is based on facts, data and research;
- is agreed by all stakeholders;
- is adaptable to change.

This checklist gives the category team an idea of what they should be aiming for when developing a category strategy. Ideally the targets that were set during Stage 1 (Initiation) should have been stretching so that the category team feels sufficient pressure to seek innovative ideas and solutions beyond the obvious.

There is nothing worse than spending three or four months of category research, analysis and strategy development only to end up with a solution that proposes to run an eRFx exercise to source a new supplier. This is not category management (it's just plain old sourcing), and it is not sufficiently challenging or innovative to add tangible 'breakthrough' value for the business. The category team needs to be far more expansive and creative in its idea generation to achieve the business requirements over a three- to five-year time horizon!

Ideas can come from a wide variety of sources, not just so-called brainstorming workshops. There is not a recommended number that you should be aiming for, but it is quite possible to have over 100 initial ideas for a category strategy. Consider asking stakeholders and consulting with the supply market, either informally through networking, or more formally through market-enquiry techniques.

Some ideas will already have been mooted by the category team during Stage 2 (Research) or Stage 3 (Analysis). These need to be recorded and stored for an initial 'sift'. Before this happens though, you should think carefully about how those initial ideas are received. It is always best to avoid early assessment of someone else's ideas, in case your rigorous evaluation leaves them unwilling to share more good ideas or, worse still, prevents someone else from sharing his or hers.

Ideas need to be worked on in order to become workable and of value. The task of the category team is to develop and refine the initial ideas by working on their practicality and utility so that they become genuine options to consider. Later in this section you will consider our option appraisal model. The difference between an idea and an option is simply one of operational effectiveness – that is as soon as an idea or concept has been assessed and sufficiently developed so that it can practically deliver the required business benefits, it becomes an option that should be appraised and tested.

As you will see in the Activity 25 (Option appraisal) later, once all options have been evaluated, the best overall option is subsequently put forward as the recommended solution.

This process of innovating and developing the category strategy is dynamic and nonlinear; it is difficult to confine to a project plan or a set of prescribed methods. One successful approach towards generating and refining ideas and options is that of 'suitability, acceptability and feasibility', which was developed by Professor Gerry Johnson et al. (2014; the originators of the PCA strategy-development model). Their methodology is based on a series of tests and refinements that take initial ideas and test/develop them first for their suitability (i.e. their ability to meet the original specified requirement). The subsequent tests of acceptability and feasibility then consider the extent to which the ideas will be embraced by stakeholders and the organisation, and ultimately the practicality and business case for such initiatives.

These tests work well in category management idea-generation or solution-development workshops and can be used effectively to develop a meaningful and value-adding category strategy.

The biggest challenge of all, however, relates to the origin of good ideas. Staring at a blank sheet of paper rarely produces valuable solutions, in much the same way as asking someone to create a valuable idea on the spot rarely generates the desired results. One tool that we have found valuable for generating initial ideas and thoughts about potential category solutions is the category strategy cube, shown in Figure 4.3.

This model provides a wonderfully rich stream of potential supply-chain solutions. It can be used in a variety of ways, from a simple checklist approach, to an analytical assessment of individual category strategies. In itself, it does not claim to generate the 'silver bullet' of a category solution, but using it within a category team will certainly generate thought-provoking ideas and concepts that will lead to a series of strategic options for the category of spend.

It should be noted that not all of the ideas and concepts within the category strategy cube are original, as there are similar dynamic models within the supply-chain community. The purchasing chessboard is one model that explores the power dynamics between buyers and suppliers to generate 64 different forms of purchasing strategy (see Schuh et al. 2012). While this is an improvement on one-dimensional sourcing strategies, it should be noted that there are serious flaws within the logic of this model (see Cox, 2014). The purchasing chessboard wrongly looks at the power dynamics of a single supplier relationship, when it should really be considering the power dynamics within the supply market as a whole. It is also limited to sourcing and process-improvement strategies, rather than considering broader business strategies for the category spend. For this reason, we consider the category strategy cube to be far more effective in helping category teams generate, discuss and refine their category strategies.

The category strategy cube has two main dimensions: one that relates to *disruptive* strategies (restructuring, supply-base leverage and product innovation) and one that relates to *adaptive* strategies (process improvement, supplier management and supply-base collaboration). There is a clear connection and overlap between some of these related strands, and so users should not get overly hung up on which strategic initiative belongs to which facet of the model.

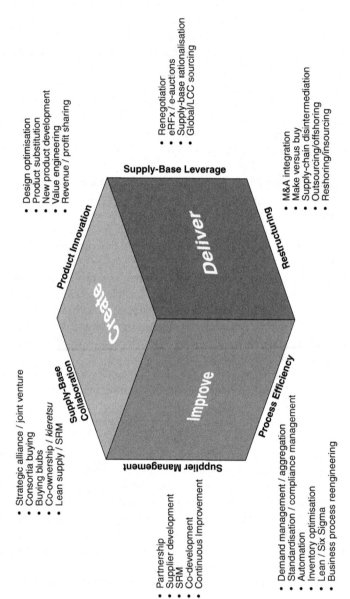

- Design optimisation
- Product substitution
- New product development
- Value engineering
- Revenue / profit sharing

- Renegotiation
- eRFx / e-auctions
- Supply-base rationalisation
- Global/LCC sourcing

Supply-Base Leverage

Product Innovation

Restructuring

Deliver

Create

- M&A integration
- Make versus buy
- Supply-chain disintermediation
- Outsourcing/offshoring
- Reshoring/insourcing

- Strategic alliance / joint venture
- Consortia buying
- Buying blubs
- Co-ownership / *kieretsu*
- Lean supply / SRM

Supply-Base Collaboration

Process Efficiency

Improve

Supplier Management

- Partnership
- Supplier development
- SRM
- Co-development
- Continuous Improvement

- Demand management / aggregation
- Standardisation / compliance management
- Automation
- Inventory optimisation
- Lean / Six Sigma
- Business process reengineering

Figure 4.3   Category strategy cube

The concept of disruptive strategy is a recognition that the status quo will be changed. This is likely to result in new operating models, business reorganisation and new upstream or downstream business relationships. Adaptive strategies, however, tend to build on the existing foundations and structures within an organisation and its supply chains.

Within the category strategy cube, there are three further features: those that *create* value (through new products and supply chains), those that *deliver* value (by changing the nature of relationships and supply chains) and those that *improve* value (from existing relationships and supply chains). The two dimensions and three features of the category strategy cube work together to form a proactive and dynamic framework for generating value-adding category strategies that look far beyond the normal remit of the procurement community.

Practical hints and tips

1 Idea generation is everyone's responsibility and involves the full category team, plus wider stakeholders.
2 Maintain an 'ideas log' throughout the category management process so that all ideas and thoughts are captured prior to assessment.
3 Do not evaluate ideas too early, and prevent any actions from occurring that could curtail the generation of additional ideas for a category strategy.
4 Use practical tools, such as the category strategy cube, to generate ideas amongst the category team and the wider stakeholder community.
5 Think beyond sourcing; there are many wider business and supply-chain solutions that you could consider that have far greater lasting impact.
6 Seek a diverse range of sources for your ideas so that the 'boundaries' of thought and innovation are stretched and challenged.
7 Once you are ready to close down idea generation, undertake an 'affinity-sorting' exercise to group together related ideas to see how these can work together and create additional synergy for the category.
8 Rigorously test ideas and options with stakeholders using the well-established suitability, acceptability and feasibility framework.
9 Be prepared to string together a series of initiatives so that a longer-term (but flexible) category plan can be developed.
10 Keep your stakeholders actively engaged throughout all of these strategy-development activities.

Summary of activities

There are six key activities outlined within this stage of the category management process:

1 **Dutch windmill** – A risk and value-based portfolio approach to the development of market-based sourcing strategies. This model offers a combination

of the Kraljic portfolio analysis and supplier preferencing matrices and indicates the relative power positions of suppliers with respect to their customers.

2 **Sourcing strategy wheel** – In many ways this model is similar to the Dutch windmill, again based on the Kraljic portfolio analysis matrix. This model helps suggest appropriate *sourcing* strategies.

3 **Power/dependency profiling** – An analytical model of the structure of power within dyadic buyer-supplier relationships. If used properly, this model helps identify the sources of power (or dependency) within a buyer-supplier relationship and therefore highlights the areas that a category strategy needs to address.

4 **Opportunity analysis and quick wins** – A simple initial 'sifting' model to separate out the higher-yielding ideas. This model can be used as an early evaluation model before ideas are worked up into fully detailed options, and it can also be used to identify 'quick-win' opportunities.

5 **Option appraisal** – This is a more detailed comparative assessment model for strategic options, set against objective criteria of 'success' (typically the business requirements) so that the most favourable option for the category can be identified.

6 **Category plan** – Detailed documentation of the category strategy, together with a plan for its implementation. This often acts as a justification and approval document for the proposed category strategy, together with a record of the research and analysis that has led to the creation of that strategy.

What the gateway needs to consider

The main goal of the gateway approval point at the end of Stage 4 (Strategy) is to make sure that all major stakeholders are satisfied with the category strategy that is being proposed. Arguably, this is the most important gateway of the whole category management process, and we would assert that it should be a clear 'go/no-go' stage gate.

There are several key questions that approvers should be asking the category team at this point, and these centre around the previous suitability, acceptability and feasibility framework outlined earlier.

One of the most significant questions is whether the proposed category strategy will deliver the stated business requirements. Asking the category team to place a confidence rating on this will help approvers decide how robust the proposed strategy is.

The following checklist gives some more practical guidance on what the category manager should be preparing for the Stage 4 gateway.

Gateway approval checklist

STAGE 4: STRATEGY

1 Does the category strategy reflect the long-term and short/ medium-term business requirements of the organisation? ☐

2 Has a wide range of potential solutions been considered for the category, including supply base leverage/collaboration; restructuring; product innovation; process improvement and supplier management, sourcing, negotiation and SRM options? ☐

3 Have all value levers been exploited for optimum value generation? ☐

4 Does the category strategy take into consideration the competitive appetite and relative power/dependency balance within the supply market? ☐

5 Will the category strategy deliver the agreed targets for the category? ☐

6 Will the category strategy deliver added value while also minimising risk and enhancing the reputation of the organisation? ☐

7 Have all social responsibility, ethical and environmental factors been included within the development of the category strategy? ☐

8 Do we have the required resources, capabilities and investments to deliver the category strategy within an acceptable timescale? ☐

9 Has an initial scan for quick-win opportunities been undertaken? ☐

10 Have all relevant stakeholders been involved in the development of the category strategy? ☐

Signed: _____

Category Manager

_____

Sponsor

Activity 21
DUTCH WINDMILL

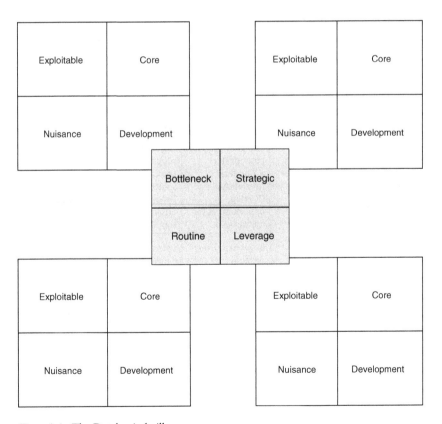

Figure 4.4 The Dutch windmill

Source: adapted from Van Weele (2014)

Overview

Professor Arjan Van Weele developed the idea of the Dutch windmill framework in the early 2000s. As a combination of the Kraljic portfolio analysis and supplier preferencing matrices, it defines 16 different types of business-to-business relationships by assessing the level of buyer-supplier interdependence that exists, together with the subsequent impact this may have upon possible category strategies.

By exploring the relationship from the perspective of both parties, it is posited that a better understanding of leverage may be gleaned, supplier-buyer collaboration may evolve and overall delivery of category management benefits, such as cost savings, will be improved.

Elements

The relationships that are produced as a result of correlating the two matrices are detailed in Figure 4.5, alongside probable actions that buyers could undertake in order to expand their overall competitive position:

	Exploit	Core	Nuisance	Develop
Leverage	Adversarial relationship Assess the power balance. Consider other resources.	Good negotiating position; improves bottom line Maximise competitive pressure on supply base.	Relationship mismatch Accept situation in the short term. Change supplier if possible.	Supplier development potential Encourage participation in savings opportunities.
Strategic	Risk of overdependency Attempt to raise the supplier's dependency. Look at alternative sources.	Complementary; potential for a long-term relationship Develop opportunities for mutual gain.	High risk of supplier exit Look at alternative sources. Become more attractive to the supplier.	Potential for a good match Work closely together to develop opportunities.
Routine	Moderate risk Review prices periodically. Review alternatives periodically.	Buyer in a strong position Maintain the relationship. Look at offering the supplier other opportunities.	Potentially a mismatch; anodyne relationship Look at alternative sources.	Supplier interest Look for further incentives to develop business opportunities.
Bottleneck	Moderate cost risk Monitor the supplier closely for price and service changes. Change supplier if possible.	Complementary; potential for a long-term relationship Develop mutually beneficial relationship to cover risk.	Disruption to service/ production risk high Change supplier if possible.	Potential for risk Work closely together to develop dependency and opportunities.

Figure 4.5 Elements of the Dutch windmill

So what?

This framework is regarded as an excellent way of 'guesstimating' the relative amount of power and hence leverage that exists within the buyer-supplier dyadic. It is held as an essential tool within the category management process and can be used to aid category strategy advancement, as well as function as an early indicator of those suppliers where the biggest benefits are likely to occur.

It also helps the category project team create a rounded view of the supply relationship, rather than a more traditional, one-dimensional perspective, and therefore may support greater collaboration between the two as appropriate.

Category management application

- Supports the development of the category strategy
- Identifies a range of likely sourcing actions
- Can support prioritisation activities
- Helps assess the potential for negotiation leverage
- Can assist the development of buyer-supplier collaboration

Limitations

This framework suffers from all of the combined limitations of the Kraljic portfolio analysis and supplier preferencing models. Although the model is particularly popular with consultants, it can become a resource-intensive exercise for practitioners, and as a result there is a tendency for some to take shortcuts in order to reduce the process, which can diminish the usefulness of the output.

For an in-depth critique of procurement segmentation models, readers should consider the writings of Professor Andrew Cox. Despite there being a few basic flaws in his arguments (as well as in the practicality of his application), there is a degree of validity in his hypotheses.

Template

The following template can be used to support the supplier segmentation process:

- Template 21: Dutch windmill

Activity 22
SOURCING STRATEGY WHEEL

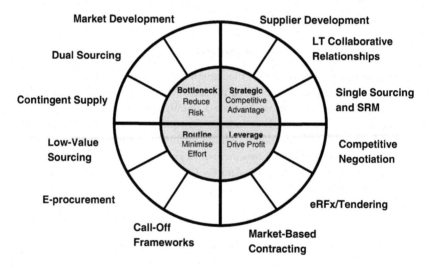

Figure 4.6 The sourcing strategy wheel

Overview

There are many options available when it comes to market engagement. Based upon Kraljic's portfolio analysis model, the sourcing strategy wheel explores the various routes that can be pursued. It was developed in order to aid category planning, and depending upon the category characteristics (e.g. high risk, low expenditure), a selection of corresponding sourcing methods is outlined.

In effect, the sourcing strategy wheel acts as a reminder of the potential points of entry on the supply side and possible mediums for implementing the category solution in the market.

Elements

The sourcing strategies are based on category positioning, which links back to Kraljic's portfolio analysis, as described in Figure 4.7.

Positioning	Sourcing strategy	Dimensions of the sourcing strategy
Strategic	Supplier development	Target: Competitive advantage Example: Where market capacity is constrained, it may be appropriate to work with a supplier to improve its offerings, rather than go back to the market.
	Long-term collaborative relationships	Target: Competitive advantage Example: Work collaboratively with an existing long-term supplier in order to work smarter and share rewards.
	Single sourcing and supplier relationship management (SRM)	Target: Competitive advantage Example: Select one supplier to fulfil entire need and work collaboratively using SRM to drive continuous improvement throughout the life of the contractual relationship.
Leverage	Competitive negotiation	Target: Drive profit Example: Use leverage and the threat of competition to achieve cost advantages.
	eRFx/tendering	Target: Drive profit Example: Use competitive quotation/tender processes to condition the market to reduce costs and offer greater benefits.
	Market-based contracting	Target: Drive profit Example: Play competing vendors against each other for short-term contracts and short-term tactical advantage.
Routine	Call-off frameworks	Target: Minimise effort Example: Use preestablished framework agreements to call off orders for standardised items as an efficient processing medium.
	E-procurement	Target: Minimise effort Example: Use a variety of online procurement and ordering tools (e.g. catalogues) to minimise transaction costs.

Figure 4.7   Elements of the sourcing strategy wheel

Positioning	Sourcing strategy	Dimensions of the sourcing strategy
	Low-value sourcing	Target: Minimise effort Example: Use a wide range of efficient sourcing methods (e.g. procurement cards) for low-value/low-risk purchases.
Bottleneck	Contingent supply	Target: Reduce risk Example: Maintain a backup 'contingency' arrangement with another (retained) supplier to alleviate risk with the existing supplier.
	Dual sourcing	Target: Reduce risk Example: Manage two suppliers in parallel to maintain flexibility and competitiveness in a difficult marketplace.
	Market development	Target: Reduce risk Example: Proactively work with suppliers (or potential suppliers) in a constrained market to develop further sources of supply and open up more sourcing options.

Figure 4.7 Continued

So what?

The sourcing strategy wheel is a useful guide to the range of potential supplier-engagement strategies available to the category manager. Undertaking supplier positioning analysis (i.e. Kraljic portfolio analysis) beforehand can be used to help develop the potential options, which means there should be alignment throughout the category process.

Category management application

• Supports the category strategy-development process
• Can gain a 'snapshot' overview of potential supplier-engagement strategies
• Helps provide a framework for less experienced category managers
• Can be aligned to Kraljic's portfolio analysis

Limitations

The sourcing strategy wheel merely acts as a checklist of potential market *sourcing* options. While it helps the user understand the selection criteria for each potential option, it does not assist with understanding how to undertake them. This is left to the knowledge and experience of the category manager, who may not be familiar with all of the ideas identified.

It should also be noted that not all of the options may be available to those working in a public-sector environment. For example, competitive negotiation may not be possible in relation to some acquisitions due to prevailing public procurement regulations.

Template

The following template can be used to identify potential solutions for your category:

• Template 22: Sourcing strategy wheel

Activity 23
POWER/DEPENDENCY PROFILING

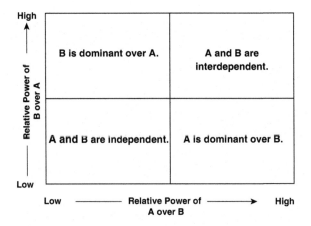

Figure 4.8   Power/dependency profiling

Source: adapted from Cox et al. (2002)

Overview

The power/dependency model charts the four potential power structures between any two parties in a commercial relationship. It recognises that both parties have elements that give them power and that therefore these respective positions need to be charted against each other.

The authors refer to these elements as 'critical assets', but they could equally include know-how, superior capabilities, market position and intellectual property.

The authors of this model claim that the power of one party over another is based on the relative scarcity and utility of each party's resources. For example, a supplier might have access to a specific raw material or design patent, which gives it relative power over a buyer.

Similarly, the buyer might control distribution to a specific market or might have negotiated a restricted covenant on a supplier's business elsewhere.

The model considers the relative strength of each party's power over the other and indicates which of the four different power structures applies in any given circumstance.

Elements

The four quadrants of the power/dependency matrix can be discussed as follows:

B is dominant over A – Party B has dominance because Party A has little or no power over it. Party B can therefore command superior terms. Typically, this could occur when a supplier operates a monopolistic market and the buyer has no practical or effective alternative.

A and B are independent – Neither party has any power over the other. This typically might be the case in low-value spot purchases within a competitive market. As such, the parties can operate with relative independence to each other.

A is dominant over B – Party A has dominance because Party B has little or no power over it. Party A can therefore command superior terms. Typically, this could occur when a supplier is dependent on a buyer for ongoing business.

A and B are interdependent – This is the situation where both parties are relatively powerful. For example, there could be contractual lock-in, intellectual property protection, restricted market alternatives and so on. As these scenarios apply to both parties, they become relatively interdependent on each other.

So what?

It is essential for buyers to understand the structure of power in any given supply-market or commercial relationship. By understanding this, they are able to determine the most appropriate category development strategy, negotiation approach and commercial terms. Put simply, without understanding the structure of power, a buyer risks being commercially ineffective.

Business relationships are becoming increasingly complex, and therefore power dimensions – and more particularly how each party uses them – are important to ensure purchasers are getting the best value for their organisations.

Category management application

- Can be used to analyse existing supplier relationships and how to manage categories of spend most effectively
- Helps with understanding supply markets prior to sourcing from them

Limitations

The authors of the model provide detailed academic descriptions of different power structures in play. However, they do not provide a succinct definition of 'critical assets', nor do they detail the way in which you can practically determine the relative power between the parties. As a result, although there is a lot of academic validity in the model, it remains difficult to apply in practice.

Furthermore, the model does not inform you what you should do in each of the four situations – and this is an essential omission in its practical application.

Template

The following template can be used to map the power and dependency structure of an organisation's relationships with key suppliers within any given category:

• Template 23: Power/dependency profiling

Activity 24
OPPORTUNITY ANALYSIS AND QUICK WINS

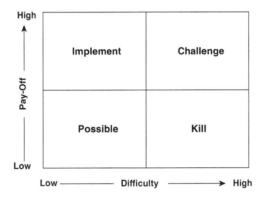

Figure 4.9 Opportunity analysis

Source: adapted from George (2003)

Overview

Opportunity analysis is a common feature of strategic planning. A number of 2 x 2 matrices have been developed by procurement consultants over the years to fit into the category management process. Most are thought to have been derived from Six Sigma's 'PICK chart', a visual tool for organising ideas and prioritising them.

At the heart of this decision tool is the equation between potential yield and effort. Therefore, in order to manage resources effectively, it is useful to apply the technique at the outset of the category management planning process, as well as during the development of the category strategy as various options arise. This way, focus will be given to those opportunities that can deliver the most benefit.

Elements

The criteria for an opportunity analysis matrix based upon the PICK principle are as follows:

- The *y* axis plots the impact of the opportunity. In procurement terms, this is likely to relate to cost reduction, improved quality, added value and so on.
- The *x* axis plots the ease of implementation. The complexity of the organisation, stakeholder willingness, skills, governance and so on will need to be considered when positioning the opportunity in line with these variables.

The four key elements of the matrix are as follows:

1 **P (possible)** – These opportunities are often termed 'low-hanging fruit' or 'quick wins'. The effort to implement these is low, but the impact is also low. These should only be implemented after everything in the I quadrant.
2 **I (implement)** – These opportunities are also referred to as 'priorities' or 'musts' and should be implemented at the earliest opportunity, as they will have a high impact and require low effort.
3 **C (challenge)** – These opportunities are sometimes known as 'back burners' or 'slow burns'. They should be considered for implementation after everything in the I quadrant, but only if a thorough assessment of the prevailing organisational climate proves positive. The impact is high, but the effort is also high.
4 **K (kill)** – These opportunities are frequently labelled to illustrate the action (i.e. 'eliminate', 'avoid' and 'don't bother'). They should be 'killed', or not implemented. The effort to do so is high, and the impact is low.

So what?

The output of the category management process should be tangible benefits to the business. Reviewing the impact of each identified opportunity in light of organisational influences can help deliver the most relevant category project within existing limitations.

The original PICK method denotes a sequence of events, and this can help the category manager plan and schedule available resources into project 'waves' of activity (i.e. Wave 1, Wave 2). Only opportunities that are regarded as implementable with a high level of return should be tackled first, as the business is more likely to buy in and engage accordingly.

However, some academics posit that reaping the rewards of less impactful 'quick wins' in the early stages of a change programme can foster immediate sponsorship and collaboration. In practical terms, it may be that these projects can deliver benefits way in advance of the larger, more complex, strategic ones. Therefore, scheduling of category team activity will need to be carefully assessed and resourced so that there is a balance between procurement and business objectives.

Category management application

- Supports an objective decision-making process
- Is a quick way of identifying category priorities
- Helps focus attention on opportunities that can deliver the most benefit
- Supports effective resource management
- Is a useful decision-making tool that can be applied throughout the category management process

Limitations

While opportunity analysis is a good visual tool for aiding a decision-making process, it is criticised for providing only a 'high-level' perspective. The current academic view is that detail relating to impact and implementation is often missed – or deliberately hidden in the case of potential issues – and inflated in terms of benefits. Thus, an unrepresentative picture of a situation can be presented.

Category managers should bear in mind that there are several ways in which the axes of the matrix can be portrayed and interpreted. Some have argued that the matrix might fare better if risk was included, while others have highlighted that the 'benefits' axis is relatively superficial and that there are far more sophisticated financial-appraisal techniques available.

When evaluating options, theorists Johnson et al. (2014) refer to three tests of suitability, acceptability and feasibility that could be considered more robust. Nevertheless, the power of the opportunity matrix comes from its simplicity, and hence this is why it has become a popular practice within category workshops.

Template

The following template can be used to chart various ideas, options and strategies on a PICK matrix and prioritise these for implementation:

- Template 24: Opportunity matrix

Activity 25
OPTION APPRAISAL

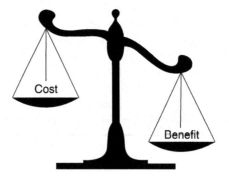

Figure 4.10 Option appraisal

Overview

The Chartered Institute of Public Finance and Accountancy (CIPFA) deem *option appraisal* as 'an essential tool to help you to deliver organisational goals'. It originated as an accounting decision-making tool that examined all available outcomes, weighing the costs, benefits, risks and uncertainties to enable an objective and systematic evaluation of the best proposal to be made.

Initial (outline) opportunities for financial benefits and other noncashable benefits are assessed using the opportunity matrix (see Activity 24). These are then refined, often on an iterative basis, so that a range of realistic, pragmatic and relevant options are established that can be compared and evaluated through the appraisal process.

It is important that the option selected by the category team be capable of delivering the output required by the initial category management programme objectives (i.e. the business requirements, RAQSCI), and in this way option appraisal distinguishes itself from opportunity analysis.

Elements

The principles of option appraisal are as follows:

- Be clear about the output desired (your objectives).
- Consider the options for achieving the objectives.
- Assess the costs and benefits of the different options.
- Quantify and value the options wherever possible.
- Consider any risks and sensitivities.
- Assess the most appropriate use of resources.

A common stepped approach to option appraisal might be as illustrated in Figure 4.11.

Option appraisal step	Activities involved
1. Focus on category management outcomes.	Review the high-level options in line with the programme objectives and business requirements (RAQSCI). Are they complementary and supportive?
2. Map the outputs of the options to the programme objectives.	Bring forward appropriate options, and detail the expected benefits in line with the programme objectives.
3. Apply weight and score.	Develop a weighted scoring methodology based on your original business requirements. Weigh the benefits of each option against the others.
4. Review the substance.	Drop any options that fail to deliver critical benefits or minimum requirements.
5. Rank the options.	Develop a ranking methodology (i.e. by attractiveness and achievability), which may be used to place options.
6. Validate with stakeholders.	Ensure continual engagement throughout the process, which should build ownership and sign-off towards this final step.

Figure 4.11 Elements of option appraisal

So what?

Option appraisal is frequently used within the procurement environment during the tender or quotation-evaluation process. The thinking and methodology used for this activity are the same in category management. It is based upon the premise that the most suitable option is selected given the criteria, which should consider both financial and nonfinancial benefits.

Each option may not need to be appraised to the same level of detail, as some may be ruled out early on in the process. Those that are assessed by the team need to be ranked, and it is often the case that individuals will need to undergo a 'standardisation process' beforehand in order to ensure consistency across the piece of work.

Ideally, all facts and data relating to the options should have been gathered and given to the category team so that the ranking process can happen simultaneously; however, practically, this may not occur, as new information can become available and therefore the process will need to be reviewed and updated.

It is essential that stakeholders are included in this process to validate the outcome and to build buy-in and commitment to the final solution. Peer review and challenge during this process can form a helpful dynamic, as they help stress-test the final option and ensure viability.

Category management application

- Supports the development of a coherent category strategy which links back to business requirements
- Provides a consistent approach to decision making
- Enables informed and transparent decisions
- Provides a clear basis for review
- Gives a clear and objective evaluation process
- Gains commitment from key stakeholders

Limitations

There is much confusion between opportunity analysis and option appraisal, and the two are often mistaken, which can lead to suboptimal decision making. Resource limitations may also dictate which documents are used/omitted from the category management process.

It is important to remember that all costs associated with the options must be included; otherwise the decision-making process will be flawed. A failure to match the option benefits back to the business requirements is another recurring theme – more commonly found in large projects over long durations.

Option appraisal is best developed as a result of team consensus; however, again, time limitations can force unilateral development of the ranking criteria, often accompanied by a financial bias which can impact upon stakeholder buy-in to the outcome.

Template

The following template can be used to support the option appraisal process:

- Template 25: Option appraisal

Activity 26
CATEGORY PLAN

Category name:	

Category scope:	Geographical coverage:

Key commercial levers:	Summary of opportunities and options:

Summary of category strategy:	

Target benefits:	$	Influenceable spend:	$

Key actions:		Deadlines:
1.		
2.		
3.		
4.		
5.		

Key risk areas:	Dependencies:

Category manager:		Category sponsor:	

Figure 4.12   Category plan

111

Overview

The category plan summarises the strategy developed by the category team and projects how the category is likely to be managed across the next three- to five-year planning horizon. As such, it is a 'live' document that needs to be updated (and version controlled) with developments as they occur within the category.

It is considered best practice to share the category plan with key stakeholders and invite continual input and feedback, so that it becomes a living document that is reviewed and updated as needed. In organisations where category management is well established, there may be a central repository of category plans that are accessible by all those impacted so they may make contributions from time to time. However, all changes and amendments to the plan should be carefully controlled and monitored.

Category managers may be periodically called upon to present their plans to their leadership team and stakeholders, inviting questioning and scrutiny. It is thought that this process tests ideas and robustness, and ultimately should enhance the viability of the strategy document.

Elements

The category plan may be used as a communication tool across the organisation; therefore it will need to be professionally presented and easy to read and follow. Typically the contents might have a structure as follows:

Executive summary – A consolidation of all salient facts contained within the plan. It should be an 'at-a-glance' briefing so that the reader can quickly pick up on key aspects of the strategy and review progress within the category.

Category overview – The type of goods/services under review, how the category is segmented, its geographical scope and top-line expenditure. This could be an abridged version of the category profile (Activity 9).

Key stakeholders – This lists the key personnel involved within the category and the potential impact of the strategy on their activities.

Analysis – A summary of the key findings extracted from the analysis section of the category management process (e.g. SWOT, STEEPLE, etc.). Supporting detail should be contained within the schedules/annex section.

Category strategy – This is a high-level view of the selected strategy or strategies, such as a renegotiate, outsource or find dual supply.

Project Plan – Key milestone activities and dates, together with resource requirements. This could also include risk and dependency flags. The detailed plan is often presented in Gantt chart format and any associated reporting documentation should be contained within the schedules/annex section.

Benefits – This lists the main benefits to be gleaned from implementing the category, together with time frames for realisation.

Implementation – This is the date for delivery/handover to a 'business-as-usual' operational environment, and so it may include a transition plan.

So what?

In addition to acting as a strategic planning or approval document, the category plan is widely used by category teams to showcase their work. If central repositories exist (e.g. an organisation's intranet), then access will be enabled for all those that maybe interested or want to contribute to the category management process.

It is useful source of consolidated information and allows the reader to gauge how a strategy may be evolving over time. It also helps the author of the document to embrace a structured approach to planning, with the added benefit of providing an audit trail of activity.

The category plan is also a great selling tool, as it evidences to others within the business the professionalism and hard work of those involved with a category management project, while providing a sense of rigour and strategic thinking behind the process.

Category management application

- Provides a consolidated overview of the category strategy
- Enables key stakeholders to view and contribute to the strategy
- Acts as a promotional tool for the function
- Is a point of continuity in the event of change in team membership
- Provides an audit trail for the project

Limitations

It is common that some form of category plan be developed by those managing the category management process; however, the size and depth of the plan will vary enormously from organisation to organisation. Some favour a very short 'one-pager', whereas others prefer as much detail as possible, which can literally run into 'hundreds of pages'. Consultants often suggest a more comprehensive version, regardless of category size; however, this can be off-putting and potentially time wasting when there is only a small value at stake.

There is also the issue of category plan presentations, which are classically held in front of a function's leadership team. These can be traumatic events for some category team members, when panel participants become too critical or opinionated rather than being constructive and helping the team to improve. From a governance perspective, these should be limited to 'decision panels'.

In short, category planning can become a prolonged industry in itself and, without active management, risks distracting from the actual job of operational execution and delivery.

Template

The following template can be used to develop the category plan:

- Template 26: Category plan

STAGE 5

Implementation

Overview and benefits of this stage

The fifth and final stage of the category management process is all about the execution of the category strategy that has been developed so far. In other words, it is about putting into practice all of the plans and activities that were signed off at the Stage 4 (Strategy) gateway.

In effect, this stage is mostly about managing change both internally and externally, project managing individual initiatives and ensuring that they are implemented and that the benefits are delivered and sustained.

Each of the activities that we have outlined in this section lead on to considerably larger topic areas in themselves. Project management and change management are candidates for separate handbooks in themselves and, arguably, if the category strategy has been as far-reaching in its breakthrough as we discussed during Stage 1 (Initiation), then significant investment needs to be made into making these strategies effective.

It is often the case that consultants for category management have been known to abandon their clients at this stage of the proceedings, leaving them the invidious task of putting into practice all of the ideas and strategies that looked so good on paper. Implementation and application are the hardest aspects of managing a category, whereas all of the preceding activities that lead up to developing a strategy effectively can simply involve hypothetical 'blue-sky' thinking and are by comparison far easier.

This stage is about actually doing the work and making the change happen. It requires robust integrated stakeholder relationships and clarity of leadership to navigate through the project plans with purpose. This is where you will find out whether you really do have full stakeholder support and supply-market leverage to implement your plans. Effectively, this is 'proof-of-concept' stage.

Needless to say, the success of this stage (i.e. delivery of the business requirements in terms of benefits realisation) rests fully on the rigour of the previous stages. Short-circuited research, ineffective analysis or half-cut strategy will immediately expose you and your organisation, so if there are any doubts, now is the time to revisit the category strategy to ensure you have 100% confidence in the success of the outcome!

Extra explanation and theory

There is relatively little new theory about this stage; it's about practical application and implementation. There are six critical steps that organisations need to work through in order to put their category strategies into effect and reap the required commercial benefits, as follows and as illustrated in Figure 5.1:

Figure 5.1   The category implementation cycle

Step 1: Category strategy – This requires the development of the overarching strategy for the category of spend in scope, as defined by the category management process Stages 1 to 4 so far. This first implementation step requires clarity of strategy and good definition in terms of a well-documented and supported rationale.

Step 2: Business acceptance – Having 'signed off' the category strategy within the category team, its steering group or the overall category sponsor, the strategy must next gain the support and 'buy-in' of the stakeholder community. This is usually internal to the organisation but can equally be extended to external stakeholders, such as customers, distributors, agents, regulators, investors and other alliance partners. It should be noted that strategy 'buy-in' is totally different from strategy 'sign-off' and requires a far more sophisticated approach to stakeholder engagement and management by the whole category team.

Step 3: Action plans – Once widely accepted, the category strategy needs to be broken down into individual, bite-sized initiatives and project milestones. These tend to have a shorter time frame than the overall category strategy and take on an 'incrementalism' approach to strategy implementation. By keeping these action plans shorter and more focused, they help maintain momentum towards the delivery of the overall strategic goals. Shorter initiatives and milestones tend to be more achievable and therefore can introduce a degree of flexibility to the overall implementation, which is essential in the modern business environment, as well as help keep the category team motivated!

Step 4: Personal objectives – Having identified individual tasks and milestones, these action plans need to be embedded into the personal objectives of those responsible (and accountable) for delivery. This creates a sense of business 'traction' on the category strategy and helps to ensure there is personal commitment from a core team for the overall implementation.

Step 5: Change management – The process of implementation is now ready to start, and change management is the underlying critical success factor within this. You will look further at aspects of change management in the forthcoming activity in this section of the handbook. It is, however, a complex and multilayered subject that requires careful planning and execution to create (and sustain) a new way of working. In general, the bigger the levels of breakthrough value that you wish to have delivered, the greater the complexity and challenge of change management.

Step 6: Benefits realisation – The final step of the implementation cycle is to reap the benefits that come from the new ways of working. Again, there is a whole activity dedicated to discussion of this within this stage of the category management process. It should be remembered that benefits are far wider than just financial, and should be built around the core business requirements that you originally identified when starting out in Stage 2 (Research) of building your category strategy. You should be aware that many stakeholders within your organisation may question the validity of the benefits if they remain intangible or ill-defined. Creating an effective measurement and monitoring system to support the demonstrable realisation of business benefits is therefore fundamental to the measure of success of your category strategy!

Practical hints and tips

1   Make sure your category strategy has very clear, defined goals and objectives that are widely understood and accepted across your stakeholder community.
2   Break down the category goals into shorter and more manageable, 'bite-sized' chunks so that implementation is easier to control.

3   Maintain open dialogue and engagement with all of your stakeholders, clearly prioritising around those with greatest influence and interest in the area of category spend.

4   Identify the drivers and values of key stakeholders so that you can harness their support, buy-in and commitment to the changes that you want to make.

5   Most people don't like surprises, so it's worth keeping an open culture within your implementation team. Clandestine approaches to change management really don't work in the modern business world.

6   Be prepared to adapt to the changing world around you (both internally and externally). This is fundamental to the success of your implementation. An agile and responsive reaction to environmental changes will help keep your strategy fresh and relevant for the business.

7   Make sure your measurement and monitoring systems for business benefits are robust and accepted by the wider business and your stakeholders.

Summary of activities

There are seven key activities outlined within this stage of the category management process. Unlike the four former stages of category management, most of these activities represent additional supporting processes:

1   **Action planning** – This is a simple but effective planning tool used for breaking down activities and projects into individual tasks and actions so that responsibilities and deadlines can be assigned and monitored.

2   **Implementing change** – The process of moving the organisation (and associated stakeholders) from the former operating model across to the new 'target' operating model. This process involves both behavioural and technical aspects, recognising that people and culture are just as important to address as the actual operational aspects of implementing the new strategy for the category.

3   **Project management** – To support the change, this introduces a fundamental set of management techniques that help implement the new operational model in a planned, timely and coordinated manner.

4   **Benefits realisation** – The process of identifying, recording, monitoring and reporting the tangible benefits associated with implementing the category strategy. While this is often financial, it does not always have to be. Improvements in customer retention, brand awareness, product quality and service delivery (to name but a few) are equally legitimate benefits that do not possess an automatically cashable sum.

5   **Continuous improvement and review** – This is the follow-up process of monitoring and enhancing the newly implemented category strategy so that the benefits gained can be built upon and improved.

6   **Supplier management** – Linked to the concept of continuous improvement, supplier management is the process of managing third-party vendors

and service providers to ensure they continue to deliver the required levels of performance that allow the category strategy to deliver the forecasted benefits.

7   **Post-Project review** – The final process of reviewing the development and implementation of the category strategy as a team and with key stakeholders so that lessons can be learned, successes can be shared and future improvements can be planned for. This process also enables the steering group and sponsor to plan the next generation (iteration) of category development, so that the ongoing continuous nature of category management is preserved.

What the gateway needs to consider

There is no gateway review for the fifth and final stage of category management, but we shouldn't assume this infers the end of the category management process. The Post-Project review activity is the last activity in the process, but as category management is iterative, it should also serve as a catalyst for scheduling the initiation of the next category management cycle in the near future and thus for commencing the next generation of strategy development.

A mature understanding of category management is that it is therefore a 'never-ending' continuous cycle of improvement and that future benefits and improvements can always be worked upon.

Activity 27
ACTION PLANNING

ID	Action	Who	When	Status
1				
2				
3				
4				
5				

Figure 5.2 Action planning

Overview

Action planning sits at the heart of category management and forms a structured approach to driving progress through the process. It is based on a simple tabulated capturing and monitoring/review of activities and tasks that members of the category management team need to complete along the journey.

Arguably this activity is not exclusive to Stage 5 but should be employed through each stage of the category management process. Indeed, if you have engaged external third-party consultants to support your development and implementation of a new category strategy, then you will no doubt be subjected to this coordinated approach of identifying and delegating actions across the organisation. Even though the consultants can overdo this in their eagerness to justify their fees, the practice is still good. Category management can be a lengthy, drawn-out process and it is easy for internal teams to 'lose their way' without organised, transparent accountability of actions, tasks and deliverables.

It is strongly recommended that a templated approach be used and that this document be kept 'live' within the shared folder that the category team accesses.

Elements

The action plan template is simple, effective and intuitive. A brief description of each of its elements can be found in Figure 5.3.

Element	Description
ID	• Each action should be numbered sequentially in chronological order from the date/time it was first created. • Once assigned an ID number, the action must always keep that ID for reference and tracking purposes.
Action	• A concise description of the required action (and deliverable) must be recorded. • Avoid jargon and acronyms; the action must be understood and unambiguous to everyone within the team and outside of it.
Who	• The name of the person responsible for carrying out the action and delivering the outcome must be recorded here.
When	• The deadline date (and, where relevant, time) must be recorded here.
Status	• The 'status' of the action must be recorded each time the actions are reviewed by the category manager. • Words like 'ongoing' are unhelpful. It is better to record a percentage completion (or similar).

Figure 5.3 Elements of action planning

So what?

As already indicated, action planning can be overdone by external consultants eager to generate a show of progress for their consulting fees. However, as a general practice, action planning is a good habit for a category team to develop. It maintains focus on the short-term, immediate activities and tasks that need to be completed, in addition to creating 'visibility' of progress for the wider team.

Action planning is essential for the category manager to maintain momentum and keep the team (and the wider stakeholder organisation) motivated towards progress.

Category management application

• Creates visibility, transparency and accountability for individual activities and tasks
• Provides a practical, structured approach for getting tasks completed
• Prevents loss of focus and maintains motivation towards short-term goals
• Provides easy and effective project management discipline throughout the team
• Helps prevent complacency

Limitations

Action planning can become overrated and 'project manager' types, who have little else to do other than fill in and review templates, obsessive. Arguably if more time was spent on doing category management rather than filling in action plan templates, then progress could be a lot quicker and more efficient.

Another limitation is the assumption that completing the action plan template is tantamount to having the action delivered and complete. In other words, the action plan itself does not get the progress achieved.

That said, action planning is a simple and effective discipline that all category teams should adopt, but it must be seen as a 'facilitator' of delivery rather than as the panacea of progress!

Template

The following template may be used to support action planning:

•   Template 27: Action planning

Activity 28
IMPLEMENTING CHANGE

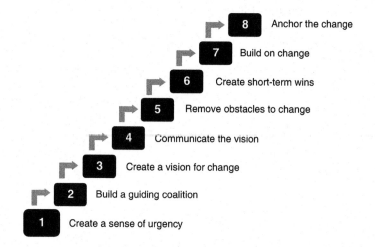

Figure 5.4   Implementing change

Overview

Theories relating to change management are abundant. Authors on the subject regularly refer to the '70% failure rate' associated with the implementation of change programmes, which essentially is what category management is about.

John P. Kotter, a Harvard Business School professor and leading thinker and author on organisational change management, developed his universally acclaimed eight-step change model in the mid-1990s. Each step highlights an important factor to be addressed when undertaking a change project.

Implementation must consider both process and people, in terms of their feelings, attitudes and mindsets. Kotter believes that behaviour is central to a successful change programme.

Elements

Category management teams can face substantial resistance to their plans from a multitude of different stakeholder groups, both internally and externally. In order to implement change successfully in a category, application of the Kotter model can help as illustrated in Figure 5.5.

Step	Description	Example of category team activity
1	Create a sense of urgency – Inspire people to move, make objectives real and relevant and create the 'burning platform'.	• Create a rationale for change. • Develop an implementation plan in conjunction with stakeholders and assign responsibilities and target dates.
2	Build a guiding coalition – Get the right people in place with the right emotional commitment and the right mix of skills and levels of authority.	• Establish an implementation steering committee, with senior support and mandate from the sponsor. • Consider using team-building exercises, briefings and so on to assist with group.
3	Create a vision for change – Get the team to establish a simple vision and strategy; focus on aspects necessary to drive service and efficiency, as well as effectiveness.	• Help the category team visualise and define what 'success' looks like, and link this into a tangible benefits-realisation plan.
4	Communicate the vision – Involve as many people as possible and communicate the essentials. Kotter's view was that programmes are often undercommunicated by a factor of 10.	• Develop a stakeholder map and communication plan, focusing on the key players. • Address peoples' concerns and anxieties openly and honestly.
5	Remove obstacles to change – Enable a constructive feedback mechanism and enlist support from leaders.	• Identify change champions who can promote positive messages. • Reward and recognise individuals who are helping to make change happen.
6	Create short-term wins – Set aims that are easy to achieve in bite-sized chunks and a manageable number of initiatives; finish current stages before starting new ones.	• Develop a schedule of 'quick wins' and promote the gains achieved through 'update' notes to key stakeholder groups.
7	Build on change – Foster and encourage determination and persistence, encourage ongoing progress reporting and highlight achieved and future milestones.	• Create a 'lessons learned' project log. • Capture ideas for improvement. • Develop a culture within the category team of continual monitoring and review.

Figure 5.5   Elements of change implementation

Step	Description	Example of category team activity
8	Anchor the change – Reinforce the value of successful change; prevent 'slippage' back into the old ways.	• Hold briefings, learning lunches, conferences, events and so on to support the change activity. Promote successes. • Develop policies and procedures to help make the change 'stick'.

Figure 5.5 Continued

So what?

Procurement functions are repeatedly criticised by other departments for placing the majority of their attention on upstream activities, such as analysis and sourcing, rather than the subsequent contract management and benefits realisation. This can lead to a 'malaise', where procurement benefits are always projected on paper but rarely delivered in practice. Kotter's framework acts as a helpful reminder of the main factors to think about when involved in the latter stages of the category management process, and when linked to best practice contract management disciplines, they can become a highly effective tool for delivering organisational benefits.

Kotter's phased model is particularly useful as it considers the representative behaviour of those affected by change at each stage and in turn how best to overcome any resultant resistance. This should aid the category team in relation to key stakeholders, who may not support or want to take on board a new contract/supplier, as ways of managing these individuals; additionally, thinking about how to demonstrate success throughout the implementation can be planned in advance.

Category management application

- Puts stakeholders at the heart of the implementation stage of the category management process
- Provides a practical, phased approach for implementation
- Considers behavioural aspects that can be helpful when working with stakeholders
- Is a useful guide for implementation activities
- Supports the benefits-realisation process

Limitations

This framework does not take into account individual capability and personality, which can have a significant impact upon change programmes. For example, inspiring and encouraging others during implementation may prove difficult for those who do not possess the necessary soft skills.

The eight-step approach also presumes a chronological flow of events. In reality, many of the change activities may be iterative or running in parallel, which means sequencing becomes complex.

The main critique surrounding Kotter's model is that it is merely a 'list', and some academics argue that it is just a part of project management, while others maintain that Kotter places far too much emphasis on changing behavioural attitudes by automatically assuming that there will be resistance regardless.

Template

The following template may be used to support the implementation part of the category management process:

- Template 28: Implementation guide

Activity 29
PROJECT MANAGEMENT

Category		Date		Owner	
Aims					
Deliverables		Quality standards			

Schedule of tasks	Duration	Owner	Dependencies

Resource	Capabilities	Availability

Communication Plan	
Risk management (cross-refer to risk log)	

Figure 5.6 Project management

Overview

Project management is the discipline applied to ensure delivery of the category strategy on time and in line with the business requirements. This could, for example, include the introduction of a new supplier, the implementation of improved contract terms or the outsourcing of an existing business process.

Arguably there are two 'projects' within category management: (1) the development of the category strategy (which we have encapsulated in Stages 1 to 4) and (2) the subsequent implementation of the solution and realisation of benefits. Both stages require project management skills to ensure timely delivery of the project objectives.

A key factor that distinguishes project management from any other kind of management is that it has a final deliverable and a finite timespan. Therefore, the category team member undertaking this role will need to have a broader range of skills due to the complexity of managing both people and process to the same end point.

A formal project management approach, together with an accompanying plan, is highly beneficial where there are numerous interdependent tasks and teams spread across several functions or companies, which are common occurrences when working within a category management environment.

Elements

A project management plan for delivering the category solution helps the team to steer a course towards its final destination. It is especially useful to have a comprehensive version at implementation stage, with the purpose being to:

- describe the aims of the implementation and expected benefits, including any assumptions or constraints in relation to delivery;
- outline the processes that will be used to monitor and report on the status, handling of risks, change progress and so on;
- ensure stakeholder buy-in and commitment;
- provide detail regarding time and dependency, for example, via a Gantt chart.

In its simplest form, project management for categories will include the following:

Project aims – The reason for the project. At implementation stage, the project aims could range from 'embedding the supplier with key stakeholders' to 'capturing cost savings through process improvement'.

Project deliverables – These are the tangible items that will ensure the needs of the key sponsors/stakeholders are met and will include time estimates, such as achieving a 10% cost savings within six months.

Project schedule – A list of individual task activities, together with how long they are estimated to take, who will complete them, any interdependencies and important milestones along the way. There are many software packages that can support this part of the plan.

Resource requirements – This is the identification of the resources required, if necessary by name or skill set, along with their responsibilities within the team.

Communication plan – Who needs to be kept informed about project progress and how this will be communicated. Normally there will be various reports with differing levels of detail for the multitude of stakeholders.

Risk management – The systematic identification, monitoring and mitigating of risks. Note that it may be necessary to cross-reference this with other risk registers/logs that may be in existence.

Quality guidelines – Assessing the level of quality required from the output. Note that the definition needs to be detailed and measurable so that achievement can be recorded and recognised.

So what?

Category management borrows many of the tools and techniques originally developed as part of the project management philosophy, mainly because of the solidity and exactitude they provide. For example, the project charter (Activity 1) and STP (Activity 13) templates create a firm foundation from which to kick off the category process.

The latter stages of a category project can sometimes be delayed, derailed or abandoned if not correctly managed, and a detailed implementation project plan will help drive results. There is an important link with 'governance' here, which relates back to all of the things you reviewed in Stage 1 (Initiation). If the category governance is set up correctly in the first place, then the implementation of the end solution is so much easier!

Category management application

- Provides a structured approach to managing the later stages of the category project
- Assigns roles and responsibilities for delivery of the category strategy
- Helps maintain stakeholder buy-in and commitment
- Supports the category management risk register and other essential governance
- Supports the benefits-realisation process
- Allows for project plans to be seen as 'best practice'

Limitations

While the ability to drive projects to their ultimate conclusion is seen as an essential competency for category managers, many fail to apply project management methodology and too often confuse planning with scheduling, when in fact both are required.

Those with a procurement background can fall short when it comes to the 'people' element of project management, tending to focus much more on the execution of tasks rather than on utilising soft skills to encourage and motivate others to achieve their deliverables, which can lead to 'change failure'.

Not adapting the project plan is also a common problem, with category managers sticking far too rigidly to the original timescales and eager to 'bank' the savings, though this may not be practicable.

Finally, one of the main reasons that project management can get overlooked is due to the crossover with governance that was addressed during Stage 1 (Initiation). This is an oversight. Project management does not duplicate category management governance; it supports and enhances it. Category teams would be well advised to overlook this essential component at their peril.

Template

The following template may be used as a project plan to support the implementation part of the category management process:

- Template 29: Project management implementation tool

Activity 30

BENEFITS REALISATION

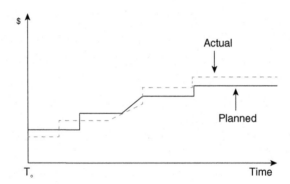

Figure 5.7 Benefits realisation

Overview

Benefits realisation is the term used to assess the level of benefits (tangible or intangible) produced as a result of implementing a category management project. Measurement of identified benefits usually occurs after project closure but needs to be carefully considered and forecast in advance. Such planning activity is usually led by the category manager in conjunction with key stakeholders who agree upon the prioritisation and timings of each of the likely deliverables, culminating in a benefits-realisation plan (BRP).

The BRP serves as a useful management tool to monitor, track and manage the collective set of benefits. It is also a way of assigning ownership and accountability to individual team members so that performance can be targeted.

Elements

When developing a BRP, it is important that all those involved agree upon the definition of what constitutes a 'benefit'. Popular terms used include the following:

Direct savings – Often refers to a cost reduction, for example, where a newly negotiated price is less than what had previously been paid. If the purchase is new, then comparisons can be made against the prevailing market rate. This type of benefit may also include retrospective rebates or contract signing bonuses. Direct savings are easily quantifiable and contribute directly to a reduction in the 'cost of goods sold'. Some refer to these as 'bottom-line' savings or 'P&L savings'.

Indirect savings – Sometimes referred to as a cost avoidance (i.e. avoiding costs that otherwise would have been incurred). Examples include negating additional insurance costs, reducing late-payment charges and avoiding price increases. These savings are valuable but do not make a positive contribution to improving the 'bottom line' and so are sometimes disregarded by finance experts.

Efficiency savings – Enables cost reduction through improved effectiveness and efficiency, such as business process improvement, inventory reduction and elimination of waste. This type of savings can be harder to quantify, but every effort must be made to translate it into a financial form so that the category team can demonstrate the value the project has provided.

Revenue generation – Where a category management initiative has helped the organisation increase its revenue income or generate new customers. These are primarily financial benefits but should be counted separately from any form of savings, as not all revenue is profitable.

Added value – Other benefits are equally important but can take a 'non-financial' form. These should not be dismissed as 'lesser' benefits; from a stakeholder's perspective, they could be more important. Typical examples include product innovation, service enhancement, risk reduction and quality improvement.

Project management authors frequently refer to a four-stage benefits-realisation process, as outlined in Figure 5.8.

Stages of developing a benefits-realisation plan	Activities involved	When during the category management process?
Identify	Assessing the benefit opportunities, reviewing the possibility of success, gauging the baseline for measurement purposes, undertaking initial prioritisation	Stage 1 (Initiation) Stage 3 (Analysis)
Define	Providing descriptions of savings, forecasting when they will be realised, outlining who will benefit and for how long	Stage 4 (Strategy)

Figure 5.8 Developing a benefits-realisation plan

Stages of developing a benefits-realisation plan	Activities involved	When during the category management process?
Plan	Detailing a project plan of deliverables, appointing roles and responsibilities for managing and tracking the deliverables	Stage 4 (Strategy)
Realise	Monitoring realisation, documenting sign-off of the benefits, integrating the benefits into 'business as usual'	Stage 5 (Implementation)

Figure 5.8 Continued

So what?

BRP is a popular category management technique that provides clear roles and responsibilities together with facilitating alignment between project outcomes and business strategies. It is believed that accountability for realisation promotes the fulfilment of the deliverables.

Research has proved that pursuing a systematic and planned approach to benefits realisation increases the likelihood of project success. In particular, continual monitoring and review is vital, as benefits may materialise throughout the project cycle and will need to be captured in order to evidence a return on investment.

Category management application

- Supports the implementation stage of the category management process
- Clearly shows who is accountable for delivery of each benefit
- Provides an overview of the projected collective benefits, together with timescales
- Helps provide category project closure
- Provides evidence of category management success

Limitations

Identification of potential savings at the outset of the category management process is perceived as essential; however, the realisation of benefits tends to be a less formal approach. In large organisations, category managers can easily lose sight of their project at the implementation stage, once it has passed into the operational, 'business-as-usual' environment. This can lead to a lack of benefits ownership, especially if it involves benefits that could take years to be realised.

It is very easy for category managers and consultants to 'overstate' a prediction of future benefits, and so enthusiasm in this area may need to be supported with rigour. Best practice is to ensure that experts from the finance department are involved in the early identification of benefits so that an acceptable measurement and tracking system can be put in place by the category team.

Ideally, a 'post-category project governance' stage, often referred to as the 'transformation committee', should be established by the category manager, but in the thrust of the day-to-day business environment, this part of the category management process can be overlooked.

Template

The following template may be used to support the identification, monitoring and review of forecasted benefits resulting from the category management project:

- Template 30: Benefits-realisation plan

Activity 31

CONTINUOUS IMPROVEMENT AND REVIEW

Category	Sponsor	CI description	Baseline	Goal	Approach (Lean/Six Sigma/Kaizen)	Status (red/amber/green)	Completion date

Figure 5.9 Continuous improvement

Overview

Continuous improvement (CI) is a philosophy that aims to ensure ongoing effort in relation to product/process enhancement. It can be termed as either 'incremental' or 'breakthrough' depending upon the scale of improvement and is directly applicable to the output solutions from a category management process, such as projects, contracts, supplier relationships and strategies.

There are many authors who have written on the subject of CI, the most notable being W. Edwards Deming, who popularised the plan-do-check-act (PDCA) cycle (a.k.a. 'Deming wheel') in the 1950s, upon which many other CI tools and techniques are founded.

Organisations undertaking CI can do so formally or informally. It occurs formally where production follows a 'lean' approach (or similar) and therefore naturally arises as part of an organisation's standard operating procedures, whereas informal CI may evolve or be included as part of a project framework.

Elements

CI activity takes place after the implementation stage of the category management process. However, it should be noted that the baseline/starting point from which CI commences will need to be mapped out as soon as practicably possible, as any gains should be measured and substantiated.

Outlined in Figure 5.10 are the most popular CI tools and techniques. They may be used in isolation or in conjunction with each other.

Tool	Definition	Application
PDCA	• Originated in the 1950s • Acronym standing for 'plan-do-check-act' • Outlines the key stages involved in the CI process	This is a helpful checking tool which uses continual review and feedback as its improvement mechanism.
Kaizen	• Based on the PDCA cycle from around the same period • Japanese CI philosophy that focuses on waste elimination from production processes	This relies upon full engagement of all those involved in seeking maximum utilisation of resources and task efficiency while maintaining quality.
Fishbone diagram	• Conceived in the 1960s by Karo Ishikawa • A popular CI tool sometimes referred to as a 'cause-and-effect' diagram	This is a problem-solving methodology that analyses the root(s) of a problem by working 'backwards' from the main issue.
DMAIC	• Based on PDCA • Acronym standing for 'define-measure-analyse-improve-control'	The DMAIC cycle is the core tool used to drive Six Sigma projects, but it is not exclusive to it and can be used as a stand-alone framework to drive improvement.

Figure 5.10 Continuous improvement tools

Tool	Definition	Application
TQM	• Developed in the 1980s • Acronym standing for 'total quality management' • Adapted from PDCA, puts quality at the heart of all processes and procedures in order to ensure a 'right-the-first-time' organisational culture	Organisational culture is driven by quality as defined by customer requirements. Top management has direct responsibility for quality improvement, which is continuously conducted throughout the organisation.

Figure 5.10 Continued

So what?

CI is an important part of category management as it facilitates double-loop learning that can create additional value for key stakeholders while providing developmental opportunities for team members. It also instils a culture of quality through continual monitoring and review activities.

CI should be regarded as a 'business-as-usual' activity, and therefore may be 'offloaded' onto those operating in the business to manage towards the latter stages of the project. However, it can be beneficial to take control of this activity as it can realise some significant benefits which may not have been previously considered in the initial phases of the category management process.

To avoid CI being overlooked and lost amongst the tyranny of 'urgent', business-as-usual activities, those organisations who adopt a more mature category management process will instil a wave-generation approach to scheduling category reviews in order to realise further additional value.

Category management application

- Provides a mechanism for continual monitoring and review
- Enables the capture and application of customer feedback
- Allows for learnings to be shared, which therefore may improve overall capability within the function
- Allows for second-, third- and fourth-generation benefits to be yielded
- Supports the benefits-realisation process

Limitations

While continually striving to improve is undoubtedly best practice, the array of CI methods and concepts available for use can be confusing. It is a very broad subject with many different schools of thought, and comprehending the multitude of offerings can be off-putting to the category manager who is simultaneously attempting to manage many facets of a category project.

It should be remembered that the focus of CI for category managers is the review and overall improvement of the output solution from the category management process (rather than improving the category process itself). There is no 'one-size-fits-all' solution and so the approach will need to be customised for each category.

It should also be noted that implementing CI requires time and effort, and sometimes resources have already been pulled from the category project as it nears the closing stages, leaving to complete the last actions only a few individuals, who may need to prioritise and therefore forego CI accordingly.

Template

The following template may be used to assist with the CI process:

*   Template 31: Continuous improvement checklist

Activity 32
SUPPLIER MANAGEMENT

Figure 5.11   Supplier management

Overview

The longer-term health and sustainability of any category solution are critical for the category team to establish before a category project is concluded. As most category solutions involve third-party suppliers, there should be a critical element within the category strategy that determines how the future solution is managed and resourced.

The category team must ensure that a detailed supplier relationship management (SRM) or contract management plan is worked through and established once the category has transitioned into its new operational environment. This will facilitate positive communication and understanding between the buying organisation and the category suppliers with regards to their roles, expectations and delivery requirements.

This needs to be done as part of the handover into the business and should consider the length, complexity and criticality of the contractual relationship, together with any ongoing issues that may arise over the term of the category solution. This will enable the most applicable form of supplier management to be put in place.

Elements

In terms of managing the supply solution once the category strategy has been implemented, it is commonly held that there are three main ways in which this might be undertaken, all of which might be applicable, or conversely just one may be adopted. Selection is dependent upon the relative importance of the supplier to the buying organisation:

1   **Supplier relationship management (SRM)** – SRM is regarded as a strategic approach to a buyer-supplier dyadic and is founded on principles such as trust, openness and continuous improvement. It centres on managing the relationship in order to gain additional value, usually from those in a so-called partnership arrangement. Not all agreements will necessitate the utilisation of this philosophy, but rather only those that are regarded as vital to the business.
2   **Contract management** – Contract management concentrates on ensuring that what was agreed by both parties is implemented and that no value is eroded, with the main driver being the contract management plan. Measurement techniques like service levels (SLs) and key performance indicators (KPIs) are instrumental to this process. There will be a far larger number of suppliers that will need to embrace this monitoring/management approach.
3   **Service delivery** – This is where implementation is carried out at 'shop-floor' level, that is between those using/consuming the product, and therefore this relies upon an operational working relationship between the individuals concerned. All contracts will have an element of service delivery, although those that are viewed as purely tactical arrangements may only have this form of supplier management in place.

So what?

A clear and concise plan that stipulates how any future supply-based solutions are to be managed is essential if maximum benefit is to be derived by the category team. In effect, implementing a supplier management approach helps make the benefits and any value added stick.

It should be remembered that supplier arrangements will vary in magnitude, and therefore an effort-versus-reward equation will need to be made so that optimum available resources may be deployed. Business participation in this decision-making process gains buy-in, which should make the adoption of any change (e.g. onboarding of a new supplier) less contentious and conflict bound.

Category management application

*   Identifies who is responsible for ensuring ongoing contract compliance and delivery

- Helps manage future supply-base risks
- Provides an opportunity for stakeholders to buy in to the change
- Identifies contracts that may be strategically relevant in the long term
- Facilitates added value and continuous improvement developments

Limitations

There is confusion amongst the practitioner community when it comes to defining the activities of supplier management. There are many different terms in existence, and this creates a problem of consistency when it comes to applying the relevant tools and techniques.

This is a wonderful opportunity for consulting companies to offer you toolkits and methodologies, many of which are unnecessarily excessive. The 'business case' for supplier management is rarely driven from any incremental cost savings; rather it is far more likely to deliver risk assurance, which means it is harder to justify on financial grounds.

In addition, it is common for buying organisations to underestimate the level of manpower required to embed supplier management. It is especially important for the category team to gain business sponsorship for critical suppliers; otherwise, continuous improvement and value-added activities can be overlooked or given a low priority.

Template

The following template may be used to support supplier management activities:

- Template 32: Supplier management review

Activity 33
POST-PROJECT REVIEW

Date	
Category	
Team Leader	
Attendees	

Areas for Review	Areas for Improvement	Actions
Process		
Resources		
Deliverables		
Timescales		
Sponsor Signature:	Team Leader Signature:	

Figure 5.12   Post-Project review

Overview

A Post-Project review (PPR) is considered 'best practice' and is often accompanied by a 'lessons learned' document. Both can help those involved with the category management process reflect upon performance and improve where possible. This learning can be shared more widely across the function/organisation so that, over time, overall category management capability and performance is increased.

The Association for Project Management advocates that a PPR is held after the handover of project deliverables and is a way of signalling an end to the programme of activities. It is also an opportunity for organisations to measure the effectiveness of their activities. This presents a challenge for 'true' category management, which should be seen as an ongoing, iterative process rather than a one-off project. Thus, for practical purposes, we recommend a PPR be conducted at the end of each category management process cycle.

Elements

Success tends to be measured in terms of the following:

- **Project delivery** – Were requirements delivered on time, on target and within scope?
- **Client satisfaction** – Were team members and other stakeholders satisfied?
- **Benefits realisation** – Did the category actually deliver the organisational benefits proposed?

In order to fully evaluate the project, the category team should come together to develop a report from which analysis can be drawn and success determined. A PPR template which incorporates a 'lessons learned' section so that participants can reflect upon performance can be used to provide structure for the review debate, as illustrated in Figure 5.13.

Report heading	Description of content	Examples of common lessons learned
Background	A brief summary of the project, including its mission, origin, purpose, business requirements and proposed end state	Business requirements were conflicting and lacked clarity.
Organisational engagement	Level of cross-functional participation, buy-in and support	There was insufficient coverage in certain business areas.
Project deliverables	A review of the outcomes in terms of planned versus actual	Most of the defined deliverables were achieved, but perhaps timescales were insufficient for scale of project.

Figure 5.13 Elements of a Post-Project review

Report heading	Description of content	Examples of common lessons learned
What went well?	Assessment of the activities, procedures and policies that went well during the process	Gateways could have benefited from more rigour.
Themes that emerged	Capturing themes that emerge as a result of analysing high-level areas for improvement	There was a lack of accurate/ reliable spend data.
Recommendations	A summary of recommendations and improvements that could be incorporated by other category managers in the future	Build more time at beginning for governance and better RACI.

Figure 5.13 Continued

So what?

The PPR acts as a final milestone in the process, and much can be gleaned from the lessons learned. If undertaken correctly, it can help others to avoid bad practice and pitfalls and can also support capability development across the organisation. For a PPR to be effective, participants need to be open about what didn't work, as well as shine a light on areas of success; otherwise only cursory progress will be made.

It should be noted that a Post-Project review is different to a 'gateway review', the latter taking place periodically in order to evaluate ongoing progress at key stages of the category management process, while the former is a one-off, single event that draws the process to a close. Best practice suggests that lessons learned be recorded as they occur during the category management process and then reviewed as part of the PPR activity, rather than held until the end of a three- to six-month process for team members to reflect on past events.

Category management application

- Provides an overview of effectiveness
- Supports a culture of organisational learning and continuous improvement
- Highlights successes and failures
- Enables development of others through 'lessons learned'
- Provides a means of self-reflection and personal development

Limitations

PPR can become a poorly executed activity for the following reasons:

- It can be difficult to maintain momentum so near the completion of the category process. As a consequence, team engagement in a review can be half-hearted.

- The quality of information extracted from the PPR relies upon the ability to draw out information that others may not want to be made public, for example errors/omissions and suboptimal practice. It is imperative that the team elects the most suitable individual for this difficult role. Good facilitation skills are essential, and it is not the case that the category manager automatically takes on this responsibility; it needs to be an independent, neutral party.

Opinion is divided amongst category management authors regarding whether to include this closure activity within the overall process. Some suggest the PPR is a necessity, while others make no mention of it at all, and therefore this lack of consistency has led to uncertainty amongst practitioners. In contrast, the 'lessons learned' concept is widely acknowledged as an important element of category management.

Another consideration is that of knowledge management and organisational learning. There is little point in undertaking the PPR activity if there is no capacity within organisational infrastructure or culture to learn from the output. It's a sobering point, but if your organisation has zero capacity to learn, then don't bother wasting your time on PPR.

Template

The following template may be used to assist with the Post-Project review:

- Template 33: Post-Project review

Templates

Project Charter

Category Project Name	Date of Initiation
Project Sponsor	**Date of Approval**
Author	**Version**

Purpose	
Scope	
Team	
Objectives	
Constraints	
Success Criteria	

Category Hierarchy

Segmentation	Key Characteristics	Similarities
Master Category		
Category(ies)		
Sub-Category(ies)		
Micro-Category(ies)		

Team Charter

Category Project Name		Author	Version

Purpose	
Scope	
Team Members	
Ground Rules	

Team Roles and Responsibilities	Team Leader Responsibilities

Risks and Constraints

Sponsor Responsibilities	
Sponsor Approval	
Date	

Template

4

RACI Chart

| R = Responsible |
| A = Accountable |
| C = Consulted |
| I = Informed |

Stakeholders

Activities and Deliverables

Stakeholder Management Matrix

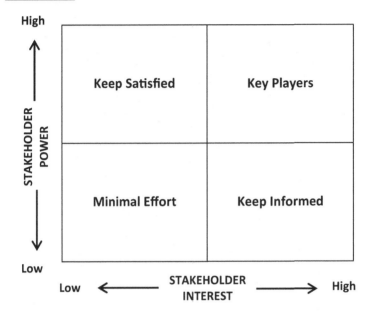

High

STAKEHOLDER POWER

| Keep Satisfied | Key Players |
| Minimal Effort | Keep Informed |

Low

Low ← **STAKEHOLDER INTEREST** → **High**

Source: adapted from Mendelow (1991)

Communication Plan

Stakeholder/ Audience	Category/ Sub-category	Communication	Method	Frequency	Owner

Risk Register

ID	Description	Impact	Likelihood	Score	Owner	Mitigation	Status

Template

8

RAQSCI

Category Team		

Author		

Business Requirement	Specific Requirements	Measurables
Regulatory		
Ability		
Quality		
Service		
Cost		
Innovation		

Category Profile

Category		Sub groups	Sites where used		Unit of measure

Total Spend	Year	Unit Price	Year	Volumes-current	Year

Current Supplier	Spend History	Potential Suppliers

Specification Current & Alternatives	RAQSCI Specification	Function of Category

Design Changes/Lifecycle	Tooling Information (if applicable)	Process Technology (if applicable)

Comments/Actions

Data Gathering Action Plan

Data	Source	Owner	Deadline

11

Key Supplier Profile

Section	Sub-Section	Information
Supplier Contact Information	Name of company	
	Address of company	
	Phone number	
	Web address	
	Key contacts/e-mail	
General Supplier Information	Company type/structure	
	Geographic coverage	
	Main sites	
	No. of employees	
Business Strategy	Vision, goals & strategy	
Financial Highlights	• Annual Sales revenues by key product ($m) • Sales	
	• Net profit ($m/%) • Profit trend	
Products and Services	Product & service offerings	
	Key markets/industry sectors served	
	Top 5 competitors	
Key Customers	Top 5 customers	
	Customer references	
	Contracts with our organisation	
	• Total spend with our organisation • Our organisation spend trend	
	Relative importance to our organisation's business to supplier	
	Supplier preferencing analysis	
	Power/dependency profiling	
Additional Info	Any other relevant info	
Summary	Implications for category strategy	

Day One Analysis

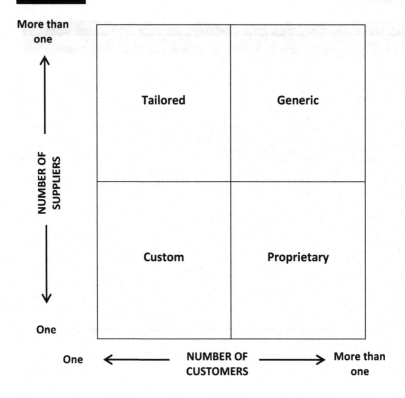

STP

Category Project		Date	
Author		**Version**	
Situation			
Target			
Proposal			

Purchase–Price Cost Analysis

Type of Product/Service	Supplier Evaluated		Date Completed		

Cost Build Up	Currency	Fixed Costs	Semi-Fixed/Semi-Variable Costs	Variable Costs	Total Costs
Labour Costs					
	Total Labour Costs				
Material Costs					
	Total Material Costs				
Production Costs					
	Total Production Costs				
Logistics Costs					
	Total Logistics Costs				
Overhead Costs					
	Total Overhead Costs				
	GROSS PROFITS				
	NET PROFITS				
	TOTALS				
			CURRENT SELLING PRICE		

SWOT

Strengths	**Weaknesses**
Opportunities	**Threats**

STEEPLE

Category		
Factors	**Comments**	**Risk of Impact**
Sociological		
Technical		
Ecological		
Economic		
Political		
Legal		
Ethical		

Porter's Five Forces

The market being analysed is:	

Competitive threat of new entrants to the market

	Summary of Competitive Position	
Is this a marketplace that suppliers want to enter? Is technological change opening up the market? Is there repaid innovation and/or high costs of keeping up? How willing are customers to adopt new ideas or new ways of working? Are there significant barriers to entry, e.g. cost regulation?	H / M / L	Notes:

Competitive threat from potential substitutes

	Summary of Competitive Position	
Are other products and services available as alternatives? Is such change likely and imminent? Is there customer or industry pressure for these changes? Are products/services being delayed for fear of impact? Are dominant suppliers actively inhibiting substitution?	H / M / L	Notes:

The bargaining power of buyers		
	Summary of Competitive Position	
Are there many buyers?		Notes:
Does demand exceed market capacity?		
Are there dominant buyers?		
Does their behaviour suit us?	H / M / L	
How restricted are buyers' choices about who supplies?		
Is our business attractive to the supply market?		
Is our expenditure attractive as a %age of market income?		
Do buyers control the distribution to end customers?		

Market Rivalry		
	Summary of Competitive Position	
Is there evidence of competition or collaboration in the market?		Notes:
How similar or differentiated are market products?		
Can the market easily find other buyers?	H / M / L	
What level of sales/marketing activity is there?		
Is there an excess or shortage of market capacity?		
What are typical profit and liquidity levels within the market?		
To what extent does the market compete on price?		

The bargaining power of Tier 2 suppliers		
	Summary of Competitive Position	
Are there many available sources of supply in the Tier 2 market?		Notes:
How openly competitive are the Tier 2 suppliers?		
How profitable and successful are the Tier 2 suppliers?	H / M / L	
How differentiated or commoditised are the Tier 2 products?		
Do a small number of suppliers dominate the Tier 2 market?		

Template

18

Supply and Value-Chain Analysis

Supply Chain	Customer	Us	Supplier (Tier 1)	Supplier (Tier 2)	Supplier (Tier 3)	Supplier (Tier 4)
Name(s)						
Role or Activity						
Value Add						
Costs						
Risks						

Kraljic Matrix

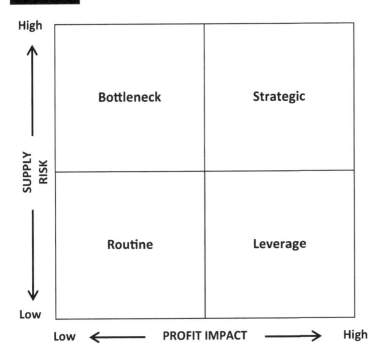

Source: adapted from Kraljic (1983)

Supplier Preferencing

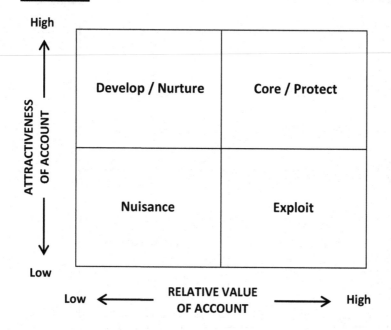

High

ATTRACTIVENESS OF ACCOUNT

| Develop / Nurture | Core / Protect |
| Nuisance | Exploit |

Low

RELATIVE VALUE OF ACCOUNT

Low ← → High

Source: adapted from Steele & Court (1996)

Dutch Windmill

Exploitable	Core
Nuisance	Development

Exploitable	Core
Nuisance	Development

BOTTLENECK	STRATEGIC
ROUTINE	LEVERAGE

Exploitable	Core
Nuisance	Development

Exploitable	Core
Nuisance	Development

Source: adapted from Van Weele (2014)

Sourcing Strategy Wheel

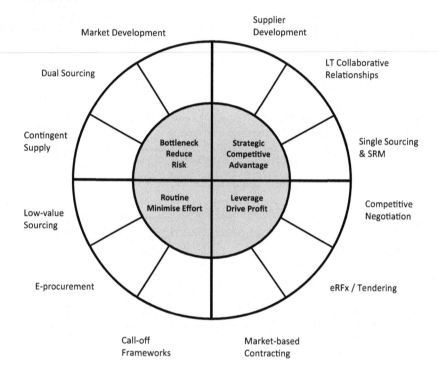

Power/Dependency Profiling

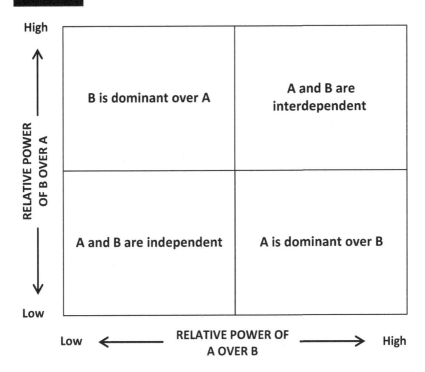

High

RELATIVE POWER
OF B OVER A

B is dominant over A

A and B are
interdependent

A and B are independent

A is dominant over B

Low

Low ← RELATIVE POWER OF → High
A OVER B

Source: adapted from Cox A.W. et al (2002)

Opportunity Matrix

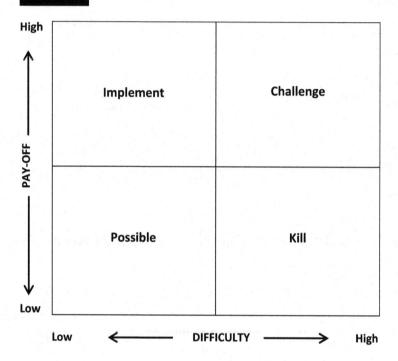

Source: *adapted from George (2003)*

Option Appraisal

		Evaluation Criteria	
	Weight	**Score (out of 5)**	**Weighted Average**
Option 1			
Option 2			
Option 3			
Total	100%		

Template

26

Category Plan

Category Name:	

Category Scope:	Geographical Coverage:

Key Commercial Levers:	Summary of Opportunities & Options:

Summary of Category Strategy:	

Target Benefits:	$	Influenceable Spend:	$

Key Actions:		Deadlines:
1.		
2.		
3.		
4.		
5.		

Key Risk Areas:	Dependencies:

Category Manager:		Category Sponsor:	

Action Planning

	Action	Who	When	Status
1				
2				
3				
4				
5				
6				
7				
8				
9				
10				

Implementation Guide

Step 1: Create Sense of Urgency

- Identify need for change?

- Identify burning platform?

- Establish critical messaging?

- Target audience?

- Deliver messages?

Step 2: Build a Guiding Coalition

- Steering committee in place?

- Senior support engaged?

- Team formation commenced?

- Team building exercises arranged?

Step 3: Create a Vision for Change

- Vision developed? ☐
- Vision understood by team? ☐
- Buy-in from team? ☐

Step 4: Communicate the Vision

- Stakeholder map in place? ☐
- Communication plan developed? ☐
- Engagement process commenced? ☐

Step 5: Remove Obstacles to Change

- Identify change champions? ☐
- Develop a feedback loop? ☐
- Reward & Recognise programme in place? ☐

Step 6: Create Short-Term Wins

- Identify 'quick wins'? ☐
- Schedule roll-out plan? ☐
- Promotions plan in place? ☐

Step 7: Build on Change

- 'Lessons Learned' log developed? ☐

- Continuous Improvement process in place? ☐

- Progress review dates in diaries? ☐

- Plan for future milestones in place? ☐

Step 8: Anchor the Change

- Bridging opportunities identified? ☐

- Rooms booked/dates in diaries? ☐

- Category policy in place? ☐

- User information available? ☐

Project Management Implementation Tool

Category		Date		Owner	
Aims					
Deliverables			Quality Standards		

Schedule of Tasks	Duration		Owner	Dependencies

Resource	Capabilities	Availability

Communication Plan	
Risk management (cross-refer to risk log)	

Benefits Realisation Plan

Benefit	Stakeholders impacted	Enablers required to realise	Current baseline measure	New baseline measure	Who is responsible	Target: Date:

Continuous Improvement Checklist

Category	Sponsor	CI Description	Baseline	Goal	Approach (Lean/ Six Sigma/ Kaizen)	Status (Red/ Amber/ Green)	Completion Date

Supplier Management Review

Criteria	Status	Action	Owner
External			
Competition Analysis			
External Environment			
Internal			
Financial Stability			
Relationship			
Technical Initiatives			
Cost Down Initiatives			
Joint Initiatives			

33   **Post-Project Review**

Date	
Category	
Team Leader	
Attendees	

Areas for Review	Areas for Improvement	Actions
Process		
Resources		
Deliverables		
Timescales		

Sponsor Signature:	Team Leader Signature:

BIBLIOGRAPHY

Butler, A.S. (1996, October). Taking Meetings by Storm. *Management Review*, 85(10), 24.

Carlsson, M. (2015). *Strategic Sourcing and Category Management: Lessons Learned at IKEA*. London. Kogan Page Limited.

Cordell, A. & Thompson, I. (2018). *The Procurement Models Handbook*. 3rd edition. Oxon: Routledge.

Cox, A. (2014). *Sourcing Portfolio Analysis: Power Positioning Tools for Category Management & Strategic Sourcing*. London: Earlsgate Press.

Cox, A., Ireland, P., Lonsdale, C., Sanderson, J. & Watson, G. (2002). *Supply Chains, Markets and Power*. London: Routledge.

Deming, W.E. (1998). *Out of the Crisis*. Cambridge, MA: MIT Press 2000.

Daft, R.L. & Lengel, R.H. (1998). *Fusion Leadership: Unlocking the Subtle Forces That Change People and Organisations*. San Francisco: Berrett-Koehler Publishers Inc.

George, M.L. (2003). *Lean Six Sigma for Service*. New York: The McGraw-Hill Companies.

Ishikawa, K. (2012). *Introduction to Quality Control*. New York: Springer.

Johnson, G., Whittington, R., Scholes, K., Angwin, D. & Regnér, P. (2014). *Exploring Strategy: Text and Cases*. 10th edition. Harlow: Pearson.

Kotter, J.P. (1999). *John P. Kotter on What Leaders Really Do*. Cambridge, MA: President and Fellows of Harvard College/John Kotter.

Kraljic, P. (1983). Purchasing Must Become Supply Management. *Harvard Business Review*, 61(5), September–October, 109–117.

Massin, J.-P. (2012) http://sourcing-and-procurement.com/

Mendelow, A. (1991). *Proceedings of the Second International Conference on Information Systems*. Cambridge, MA: SMIS.

Nielsen, A.C. (2006). *Consumer-Centric Category Management: How to Increase Profits by Managing Categories Based on Consumer Needs*. Hoboken, NJ: John Wiley & Sons Inc.

O'Brien, J. (2015). *Category Management in Purchasing: A Strategic Approach to Maximize Business Profitability*. 3rd edition. London: Kogan Page Limited.

Porter, M.E. (1980). *Competitive Strategy: Techniques for Analysing Industries & Competitors*. New York: The Free Press.

Porter, M.E. (1985). *Competitive Advantage: Creating and Sustaining Superior Performance*. New York: The Free Press.

Project Management Institute. (2017). *A Guide to the Project Management Body of Knowledge (PMBOK® Guide)*. 6th edition. Newtown Square, PA: Project Management Institute, Inc.

Schuh, C., Raudabaugh, J.L., Kromoser, R., Strohmer, M.F. & Triplat, A. (2012). *The Purchasing Chessboard: 64 Methods to Reduce Costs and Increase Value With Suppliers.* 2nd edition. London: Springer.

Steele, P.T. & Court, B.H. (1996). *Profitable Purchasing Strategies.* Singapore: McGraw-Hill.

Taylor, M. (2013). *Who Killed Category Management: What Every Salesperson, Marketeer, Retailer and Shopper Needs to Know About Retail Shopper Management.* Charleston, SC: CreateSpace.

Tuckman, B. (1965). Developmental Sequence in Small Groups. *Psychological Bulletin,* 63, 384–399.

Van Weele, A.J. (2014). *Purchasing and Supply Chain Management.* 6th edition. Hampshire: Cengage Learning EMEA.

INDEX

Printed in the United States
by Baker & Taylor Publisher Services